This is what people are saying about Playing with Fire

"An absolute winner! It should be on your must reading list!"

Norm Sonju, general manager, Dallas Mavericks

"Jay's writing style makes for fun, easy reading. What Francis Schaeffer might call the self revelation of the immutable, eternal "I Am," Jay boils down to simply "God stuff." But don't for a minute think the content is superficial, it's not. This book is a thorough systematic theology on heaven and hell written for those of us who shy away from books with titles like *Systematic Theology*."

Dana Key, musician; vocalist; concert and recording artist

"All who are truly concerned about the hereafter will find the concepts presented in this book both enlightening and provocative."

John Wooden, UCLA basketball legend

"For those of us with an unsaved parent, relative, or friend, I can't think of a better book to put in their hands. I know. With my father dying of cancer, I thank God I had this book to give him as he struggled over committing his life to Christ.

"Leave it to Jay Carty to lay on the line the life-and-death issues of salvation. In a humorous, compelling, convicting way, he can grab a loved one's attention who needs to know Christ—and bring them face to face with the Savior."

John Trent, Ph.D., vice president, Today's Family

"*Playing with Fire* is vintage Carty. Intellectual apologetics this is not. Airtight theological arguments? No. Jay is his own art form. He gets you dying of laughter on one line, afraid of dying on the next. Herein discover a creative mix of fire and brimstone with the flavor of friendship evangelism. Please, friend, take this truth to heart— your life depends on it. Spend some time getting found (not lost) in these pages."

Tom White, Frontline Ministries

"To springboard into the deep water of difficult Bible theology without drowning in the process is a monumental feat. But Jay Carty got me so involved in the action of the book, I could hardly lay it aside. One moment I was wiping tears of laughter; the next I was wincing with conviction for my own casual attitude about the eternal destiny of those around me. Jay says it like no one else can or probably should! Read it!"

Bob McDowell, executive director, Warm Beach Camps

"Jay Carty combines compassion, tough-minded insight and gives answers through stories, humor and God's Word."

Gary Lydic,
director of ministry services, Focus on the Family

"It is fascinating to read old truth in a fresh, new way. You will find this book to be interesting, up to date, and current in its presentation of complex, timeless truth. The style is twenty-first century, the truth is first century, and that's a good combination for the '90s reader who desperately needs answers to the greatest questions of the ages. Jay Carty finds the answers in the Word of God—the only place they are reliable."

Tim LaHaye, president, Family Life Seminars

"What is the value of a soul and how is the value determined? Jay's answer to this question is worth the price of this book. And if you ever doubt that our loving God would actually allow good people to go to hell, you'd better read it."

Gene Head, Menninger Youth Advocacy Project

"Thanks, Jay, for striking my awareness. I truly believe that for all who read this book, it will have a major impact on what they do with the rest of their lives."

Jerry Colangelo, president, Phoenix Suns

"If the purpose of the pastor is to comfort the afflicted and the point of the prophet is to afflict the comfortable, then Jay has been busy at both ends of the court."

Tom Hemingway, center director,
Spring Canyon Lodge, Officer Christian Fellowship

"Jay Carty . . . what can I say? He is a totally unique man with a totally unique ministry who has a totally unique gift of making some of the heaviest truths in Scripture understandable and relevant."

Ken Poure, director-at-large,
Hume Lake Christian Camps

"Don't be fooled by creative word pictures and titles that snap, crackle, and pop. Underneath the artistry of a master wordsmith is a sobering message: Nice people really do go to hell.

"The Bible doesn't stutter when it addresses the issues of heaven and hell. They both are real places and will be populated by real people, like you and me. Jay Carty, never one to hesitate to break in where angels fear to tread, has done the church a great service by reminding us that many who think they are going to heaven aren't. In his book, the author brings the *h* word out of the closet and confronts the reader with its sobering implication."

Joe Aldrich, president, Multnomah School of the Bible

"This book torpedos the comfortable assumptions so many people make regarding who ends up in hell. It's entertaining, biblical, and very frank."

Chris Adsit, president, Disiplemakers International;
director of training, Athletes in Action

"This book is great and has stirred me to tears more than once. The reality of where my old workmates are going to spend eternity has hit home hard. At last I've found a book that I can confidently hand to a friend without them thinking I'm preaching at them."

Owen Tasker,
Dallas Theological Seminary student, New Zealand

"Jay Carty powerfully challenges the all-American myth that solid citizens impress God enough to change his rules about heaven and hell. *Playing with Fire* is a fascinating book of dread reality and enormous hope."

Bruce McNicol, president, Interest Ministries

"I was a soldier for over thirty years. I know what war is. Hell is hell, so is war. But hell scares me a lot more than war. This book is a battle cry. Jay has motivated me to tell the nice people I know about the horror of hell and the possibility of heaven. The battle is joined."

Don Snow, lieutenant colonel, U.S. Army, retired

"Once again, Jay's unique and humorous writing style has brought fresh understanding and clarity to a subject that is uneasy and unsettling. This book forces all Christians to evaluate how we live our lives. It has also caused me to reevaluate the mission of our church, because if we really believe nice people do go to hell, wouldn't we do church differently?"

C. Glenn Sauls, senior pastor,
First Assembly, Asheboro, North Carolina

"If people believed in hell as much as they use the word, there would be a lot more of them going to heaven. Jay has creatively put together a number of excellent illustrations to confront us with the reality of hell. He logically points out the absurdity of believing that just being good or nice will get someone into heaven. By the time you finish this book you will know heaven is open to all, but only according to God's plan."

Doug Childress, president, Staco Corporation

"I really enjoyed this book. What I appreciate about Jay's approach, aside from his demented sense of humor, is his reliance on the Word of God as the final authority."

Paul Westphal,
N.B.A. All-Pro, Head Coach, Phoenix Suns

"Once again our friend, Jay Carty, has told it like it really is. His wonderful sense of humor and ingenious way of illustrating scriptural principles makes it a little easier to see ourselves as we really are. We are challenged and encouraged by this new book and will be recommending it wherever we go!"

Norm and Bobbe Evans, Pro Athletes Outreach

"Buy this book! Give it to someone you love and would like to see in heaven! Jay writes like he speaks—entertaining but with eternal consequences!"

Edward F. Stevens, President
George Fox College

"Jay Carty's unique style brings theological truths in language that is the language of today. You will be fascinated with this book that takes an uncompromising and hard-hitting approach to our biggest problem."

Dennis A. Davis, President
Northwest College, Kirkland, Washington

Playing with FIRE

JAY CARTY

PLAYING WITH FIRE

Published by Yes! Ministries
1033 Newton Rd.
Santa Barbara, CA 93103

Edited by Steve Halliday
Study Guide by Sam Talbert

Printed in the United States of America.

Library of Congress Cataloging-in-Publication Data

Carty, Jay.
Playing with Fire: do nice people really go to hell? / by Jay Carty
p. cm.

1. Hell—Christianity 2. Christian life—1960- I. Title.
BT836.2.C378 1992
236'.2—dc20 92-18733
CIP

CONTENTS

DEDICATION AND ACKNOWLEDGMENTS

I was doing lunch with a friend back in 1982. He told me about a message his pastor had given titled "When Are We Gonna' Believe That Nice People Go to Hell?" It hit like a ton of bricks. I wrote the concept down on a napkin and gave it some serious thought. This book is the result.

Don Roberts, please accept my thanks for the concept. This book is dedicated to you.

I also dedicate this book to Chuck Kelley. It was Chuck who reminded me ten years later where the idea came from.

My thanks to those who helped with manuscripts: John Trent, Chuck Kelley, Sam Talbert, Sarah Hemingway, Paul and Cindy Westphal, Swen Nater, Norm Sonju, and Jack and Melanie Glubrecht.

My "Paul," Sam Talbert, wrote the study guide. Thank you, Sam.

INTRODUCTION
A Lesson in Gambling

What really happens when we die?

Do we cease to exist as an entity?

Do we all go to heaven?

Is there a place called hell?

If I'm a good person do I have to worry about hell?

If hell is real, how good is good enough to not go there?

Do nice people really go to hell?

So many religions. So many beliefs. Who is right? Is anybody wrong? Is having any faith good enough as long as it's sincere? Can we know for sure?

Most people believe if they're a good person they'll be okay. What do you think?

I won't attempt to prove anyone right or wrong in this book. However, I will attempt to establish some probabilities. Odds are something I understand. My dad was a bookmaker and gambler for part of his life. He even made a living playing poker. I was raised in the world of gambling.

One thing I learned was—don't bet too much on a long shot. Long-shot gamblers are losers. For every person who wins the lottery there are millions upon millions who don't.

I'm not in favor of the lottery, but I understand the concept. Long shots can be fun if there isn't much at risk. Why not spend a buck you don't really need if there is a small chance of winning millions? However, with the probabilities of winning the lottery would you bet your monthly paycheck? Some people do, and we call them addicts and try to get them to go to Gamblers Anonymous. A person who would risk the equity in his home would be sick and we would encourage him to seek treatment. A person who would bet his life would be called suicidal and placed in a padded cell.

What would you do with a person who honestly concluded the odds on the Bible being wrong were like those of winning the lottery and still bet their soul against it? Most people do nothing. It's strange that we would pressure a gambling addict to get help because he is depriving his family of his paycheck and risking their well-being. We have made taking your life against the law to help deter suicides. But we do little or nothing for those who defy the odds and place their eternal souls at risk.

You wouldn't buy a stock the experts said was going to decline in value unless you were convinced it was going up. You wouldn't purchase a home in a declining market unless you thought things were going to turn around. However, you would need some pretty good information to go against the pros and buck the odds, wouldn't you? How good is your information regarding eternity? Are you going on a gut feeling or what someone told you? Are you going on something a teacher or professor taught you in school? Is your source more reliable than the Bible? Consider what's at stake. What if you're wrong?

You wouldn't risk your life to save another person without estimating your chances of survival. There isn't a student in the world whose teacher grades on the curve who doesn't look around the room and try to figure the odds of getting the grade they desire. *What are my chances of...?* You fill in the blank. We are always balancing upside potential against downside risk. We do it all the time—except when it comes to eternity. Then, for some reason, most people throw the odds out the window and stick their heads in the sand and call their decision intelligent.

There is a question that I'll deal with in the last chapter that I'd like to ask now:

> *With what you know about the Bible, what are the odds of its main themes being wrong?*

If your beliefs are contrary to the Bible, what are the odds of you being right? How much of a long shot would betting against it really be? You won't know my answer until chapter eleven, but keep the question in the back of your mind as you read.

What I'd like to do in this book is tell you the way things will be if the Bible is correct. Then in the last chapter I'll establish the probabilities of the Bible being right or wrong. Then you'll be in a position to make your bet intelligently. By then you will have some idea of the odds. Just remember your soul is on the line.

Most are betting eternity on the basis of how "good" a person he or she has been. The majority of people do not believe nice people really do go to hell. That's true of Christians as well as non-Christians. However, I am convinced the evidence supports the following conclusion:

Whether a person goes to heaven or hell depends on something other than how they lived their lives.

If that statement is true, being nice won't have much to do with what happens next.

I'd like you to come to grips with what happens when you die. Heaven or hell? Interestingly enough, when telling us about eternity, God spends two-thirds of His time on hell, and only one-third on heaven.

Of course, none of this makes any difference if heaven and hell aren't real. But what if they are?

What if the whole deal is real?

The deal I'm referring to is this Bible stuff. God, Jesus Christ, heaven, hell, eternity . . . stuff like that. What if it is true? What then?

We'll find out if the whole deal is real when we die, that's for sure. But can we know before our demise? That's why I wrote this book.

Death as the end is really just a beginning, so it's a good place to start. Chapter one is about death. Fun!

Chapter One

WHY DREAD DEATH? (Is the whole deal real? We'll know when we die.)

I served as an assistant coach at UCLA during the golden years of the reign of the legendary John Wooden. During my first year I assisted Gary Cunningham, the freshman coach. My job was to work with Lew Alcindor, later to be known as Kareem Abdul Jabbar. Some consider Kareem to be the greatest basketball player of all time. My second and third years on staff, in addition to coaching, I scouted and got involved in recruiting.

Like most big universities, UCLA subscribes to several scouting services. These agencies provide rundowns on key high school players around the country. Our policy was to send letters of inquiry to the highest-ranked ones to see if they had any interest in the Bruins.

One response came from Franklington, North Carolina. Henry Bibby was six feet and two inches, fast, could dunk, was averaging thirty-four points per game, and was supposed to be a terrific outside shooter. My job was to evaluate him, and if he looked good, try to interest him in UCLA.

As a struggling graduate student, I didn't have much

money. But a wealthy Bruin booster who was my size gave me his hand-me-down suits. He only wore them a few times, so I had some mighty fine threads. The slang term that described me at the time was "clean."

I put on my shiny gray, silk sharkskin suit, added a pink tie with black polka dots and headed for the heart of A.C.C. (Atlantic Coast Conference) country. I flew into Raleigh, North Carolina, rented a big high-performance muscle car (they were a big deal in the late sixties) and headed out to Franklington.

In those days in that part of the world, there were two schools in every town—one white, one black. Racial prejudice was overt and the Ku Klux Klan was active. The principal at Henry's school was a great guy and showed me the Klan flyers he regularly received as an attempt at intimidation. I met Henry's parents and we enjoyed each other instantly (that's important to a recruiter).

The game that night was a blowout so I couldn't tell how good Henry really was. He was playing two days later in a town forty miles away where his aunt lived. I made an appointment with the family to meet at her house after the game.

They warned me not to be late. The gym was small and there would be an abundance of coaches around trying to get to Henry, so there wouldn't be much room. Naturally, I got lost.

As I finally found this little town I was desperate for directions. I came across an old gas station. This place was so old the pump had a five-gallon glass globe at the top. The user would hand-crank gasoline up into the globe and then turn a lever to release the fuel into the car. A pickup truck with a rifle hanging in the rear window was parked outside.

Inside, three men in overalls were sitting around a pot-bellied stove, chewin' tobacco and spittin.' One was fat, the second was skinny with a huge Adam's apple and no chin, and the third was kind of nondescript. They were wearing baseball hats and smiled as I walked in, showing the kind of mouth of which a dentist would say, "Your teeth look great, but your gums will have to come out." These men were classic rednecks and they were staring at my tie.

"Could you give me directions to the black school," I innocently asked, never imagining their response.

They all stood in unison, moved toward me, and started mouthing off. To make a long story short, they hassled me for a while but finally grunted and pointed.

The game was a sellout. The gym was so small, even standing room was gone. Several people were doing their best to watch the game from outside through the front door. I was in trouble.

It was then that a little girl grabbed my hand and asked, "You're Mr. Carty, aren't you?"

"Why yes!" I was surprised. "How did you know?"

Without saying a word she looked at my tie, smiled, and led me off through the crowd.

UCLA had won an unprecedented number of championships and ESPN had not yet given lopsided exposure to the eastern schools. We were a very big deal in those days. Apparently everyone knew the man from UCLA was in town.

As I was escorted into the gym, the crowd instantly knew I had arrived. The game continued, but all eyes watched the shiny gray, silk sharkskin suit and the pink tie with black polka dots as I followed this darling little girl along the sideline to mid-court where Mr. and Mrs. Bibby had saved me a seat.

Do you understand what it means to have the key player's folks save you a seat when there are sixty coaches in the gym? I looked around and saw them staring with envy like starving piranhas. Picking out the coach from North Carolina, I put my hand over my face as if to say, "Face!" I looked at the coach from Duke, smiled triumphantly and thought, *Take that!* I looked at the guy from Wake Forest and just snickered. Things were looking pretty good. Henry was a great player.

After the game we went to the aunt's house on the black side of town and talked about UCLA and Henry's future as a basketball player. As it turned out, Henry Bibby played a big part in bringing the Bruins three more national championships, and he went on to play nine years in the NBA.

But this story is really about what happened after the meeting. It was 3:00 A.M.

There was an unwritten rule in that part of the country. No whites in the black part of town after midnight. The rule was enforced by whites, not blacks.

As I got into my car, headlights came on behind me. Pushing the pedal to the metal I peeled out and started roaring out of town at almost ninety miles per hour—and still I wasn't losing the headlights in my rearview mirror.

Maybe I forgot my wallet and Mr. Bibby is trying to catch me, I thought. Reaching for my pocket I knew that wasn't true. Maybe I forgot my coat. Nope. I was wearing it.

All I could think of was those three rednecks from the gas station, that pickup truck, and me being a West Coast guy alone in the middle of A.C.C. country. I was scared. Perhaps as much as I have ever been. I didn't know what was going to happen and I was afraid.

What You Don't Know Can Scare You

Nothing is as sure as death and taxes, they say. Well, I don't know who "they" are, but they're wrong. I know people who don't pay taxes. But there is one thing that's for sure: Death! And I don't know anyone who either hasn't had to or who won't have to die. Do you?

Death is something we'll all face, and it's scary. What's next is an unknown, and the unknown is a scary place. That's why I step on spiders. *I'm afraid of you.* Smoosh! Isn't it the same for you?

We tend to avoid situations where we don't know the outcome. The unknown is disconcerting and we become fearful. It's almost a universal truth. Of course there are a few who thrive on the exhilaration of the unfamiliar. The ones who like to walk on the edge. Rock climbers, sky divers, and bungee jumpers are all in that category. But remember, even daredevils are aware of their odds and the probabilities of survival. They rarely spend much time thinking about the possibilities of death, because they aren't doing it to die. They're doing it because it's fun. But death is the one unknown that brings fear into even the most courageous of characters. Look into a daredevil's eyes after one of his friends has died. You'll see fear lurking there.

Death: The Ultimate Unknown

A great rabbi was on his deathbed in the final minutes of his life. "How do you feel?" asked his concerned son.

"How do you think I feel?" replied the frightened old man. "I'm about to find out if what I've believed all my life is true." The man was afraid. Death can do that to a person.

Thirteen years ago I was running a Christian conference center in the mountains of Southern California. A woman in her early fifties, suffering from emphysema, went up to her cabin to get her Bible, came back down, and then went up to the chapel for the meeting. Keep in mind this camp was at 5,500 feet elevation.

I happened to be in the chapel when she and her two lady friends arrived. Complaining of dizziness, she clutched at her friend's shoulder and fainted. I caught her just before her head hit the cement.

She revived quickly, but I asked Jim Johnson, the assistant manager, to get the camp van anyway. I thought a trip to the hospital was in order.

I ran down to the office to get the insurance forms and was standing in the street when Jim arrived with the three ladies in the back. One of them screamed, "She's stopped breathing!"

The other chimed in, "And I can't get a pulse!"

I jumped in the van, wedged myself tightly and asked, "Do you know CPR?"

One of the ladies screamed in panic, "No!"

"Then pray."

The other friend yelled over the noise of the accelerating van, "I do."

"Then you start chest compressions. I'll do mouth-to-mouth."

Don't let folks tell you that a rubber dummy is anything like the real thing. It's not. You can't duplicate the emotions of life-and-death encounters in a teaching session on a Recessa Annie. A sense of panic grips way down deep. And there is overpowering fear. *What if she dies?*

I rocked her head back, fished for her tongue with my fingers, cleared the airway, took my breath for two, clamped down with my lips, made the seal around her mouth, and blew.

The bond wasn't tight enough and the air escaped out the sides of my mouth. *Oh no, what if she dies because I didn't do it right the first time?* My fear was showing. I had to suppress panic.

The second time I pushed down hard around her mouth and blew. Her chest elevated—I was doing it right! But after seven more puffs nothing was happening. *Am I breathing for a dead person?* I wondered.

Normally it is a twenty-minute ride to the hospital. We made it in fourteen. My knees were getting raw from sliding on the metal floor, but I didn't notice. The ninth puff brought her back.

Words can't describe my relief. Holding my ear to her mouth, I listened to make sure her breathing continued. Twice more she would stop. But one puff brought her back each time. And by the time we arrived at the hospital, she stood up and walked in as if nothing had happened. Shock is a strange phenomenon.

The rest of us were wrung out. The intensity of the situation and the fear of death had taken its toll.

By the way, the next day at camp I was naughty. The lady knew I had gone mouth-to-mouth with her. When we saw each other I told her, "When I clamped down on you I think you kissed me back. And it was pretty good, too." Although the poor woman couldn't look at me the rest of her time at camp, I found out later she thought it was funny. We had cheated death—but only for a few years. She was still going to die . . . sometime.

So are you.

Looking Death in the Eye

Have you ever seen a dead body? My first encounter came when I was in sixth grade. My dad and I were in the High Sierra fishing for golden trout. We had come into the high country via a light airplane. The landing strip was noted to be very difficult and wasn't a place for beginners.

Later the next day a plane tried to land, but it came in too high and too fast. The pilot flew out the end of the canyon, circled all the way around and tried again fifteen minutes later (it took that long to make the circle). Same problem. He was too high. But instead of flying all the way around, he turned around in the wide end of the canyon and flew back trying to land from the wrong direction. Again he overshot the runway, only this time he flew into the narrow, steep-walled, box canyon from which there was no way out.

Tiny, the three-hundred-pound camp caretaker, hollered, "Get the buckets and the shovels. I've never seen anyone make it out of there yet."

As I watched, the plane went to the far right of the canyon wall, utilizing all the space it could, did a hard turn to the left, but stalled and did a wing-over into a large pine tree. Fire and smoke were instantaneous. Within minutes we were on our way to fight fire.

When we got there I could only see two dark shapes—one in the wreckage in the midst of the fire, the other off to the side. I was on the water detail.

After a long night with many thoughts and very little sleep, my dad and I had the morning watch until the coroner arrived. There was a tarp with two shapes under it. I walked by several times, looking and wondering. My father finally said, "You'll have to face death sometime. If you want to face it now, we'll do it together.

If you want to wait, that's fine too. It's your call."

It took another half hour for me to make up my mind. Death is such a scary thing. Dad pulled back the corner of the covering and I saw the great fear-maker for the first time. Death and I had looked at each other face to face.

Have you looked death in the eye?

The Harsh Reality of It All

Some people say death won't be so bad—it's how you die that's scary. But I don't know if that's true. When you take a corner too fast in a car, what happens to your stomach? It flip-flops. Why? Death is a frightening prospect. When you're alone in your house at night and you hear a strange sound, why does the adrenaline shoot through your body? Because you are scared out of your gourd. Why? Death is scary. You may tell me or yourself you're not afraid of death, but your stomach will give you away every time.

> *If the possibility of death scares you, deep down, what must its certainty do to you?*

Dying is unavoidable and it's scary. However, the Bible has much to say about death so we need not fear it.

I love the way the apostle Paul faced death. The Romans imprisoned him and threatened, "We're gonna' kill ya.'"

"Great!" hollered Paul. "I'll be with the Lord in Paradise."

"Well, since you want that, we're not gonna' do it. Nope, we're gonna' torture you instead. Whadda' ya' think of that, wise guy?"

"Wonderful! I'll identify with the sufferings of my Lord. Just be creative."

Perplexed, they threatened to chain him to a guard and rotate the jailer every four hours.

"That's the best yet," was Paul's ecstatic reply. "What a great witnessing opportunity. It takes me about that long to explain thoroughly how to be born again."

What do you do to a guy like that? Anything! Nothing! The Romans couldn't figure it out either. So they turned him loose.

Paul was ready for death. You can be too . . . unless you are planning on beating the odds.

What Are Your Odds of Not Dying?

Name two Old Testament characters who never had to die. If you said Enoch and Elijah, you have been raised in Sunday school. Well, if you think you're so smart, try this question. Who were the three most righteous Old Testament saints? I've had only one person ever answer this one correctly. Do you know? Go ahead, take a guess.

Did you say Abraham? No, he slept with Hagar.

Moses? Naah! He killed an Egyptian.

David? Are you kidding? He committed rape, adultery, and murder.

How about Myshack, Yourshack, and Abungalo? Nope! None of those guys.

The three righteous Old Testament saints are found in Ezekiel 14:14: Noah, Daniel, and Job. It surprised me, too. But as good as they were, did those three guys have to die?

Sure they did. They died just like everybody else. Only Enoch and Elijah escaped death.

Who's the greatest man ever born of a woman? Jesus

said it. Yes, John the Baptist. Did he have to die? Yep!

Jesus raised three people from the dead. Who were they?

The most widely known is Lazarus. You probably know the story.

Lazarus had died. They wrapped his body in cloth and burial spices and put it in a tomb. Three days passed. The weather had been hot and steamy so Lazarus was real ripe and smelly. Martha knew what it would be like so she hollered to Jesus, "Oh Lordy, don't go in there, by now he stinketh to high heaven, if You'll excuse the expression."

Even in King James language Jesus knew what she meant, sniffed the cave once, caught her drift (or her brother's), and took her advice. *Peeuuuuu, I'm not going in there* He thought. So Jesus yelled, "Lazarus come forth." And he did. (You probably didn't know there were three other guys in there with him. It's the only way Lazarus could have been fourth.)

Who were the others Jesus raised from the dead? Jairus, the synagogue official, had a daughter whom Jesus brought back to life. The third one was the widow's son. Remember him? That's a great story.

In those days, it was necessary to hire at least three mourners for a funeral, even if you were poor. They were each paid a dead pigeon.

Picture the mother of the dead boy leading the parade, followed by three wailing old women faking it. (You couldn't get much for a pigeon, even in those days.) They were followed by several men carrying a box, with no lid, containing the body. The corpse had been wrapped and spiced, just like Lazarus. The men were followed by other family members and interested people.

Jesus was on the road walking toward the funeral

procession. He passed by the mother, continued past the mourners, walked up to the men carrying the makeshift coffin on their shoulders (*This will be fun*, He thought as a smile curled at the corners of His mouth), and then touched the box. Hey! The kid sat up. Whoa! The men were so scared they dropped the box, which killed the kid, and Jesus had to raise him a second time. No, no, no, I'm just kidding about the men dropping the box. But I'll bet they were pretty freaked out.

Did those three people—Lazarus, Jairus's daughter, and the widow's son—have to die again? Yes, they did. Even though they were brought back to life, they had to die again. So did the one the apostle Peter brought back. The prophet Elijah brought a boy back to life, but the kid had to die again, too. God used both of those guys to bring people back to life. The disciples were able to do it too. But everyone who cheated death once ultimately croaked for good. Except Enoch and Elijah.

What are your odds of being like Enoch and Elijah? Not very good, are they? So you might as well face it. Unless you end up like "E-1" or "E-2," you are going to die.

But what happens next? Billy Graham said, "It becomes increasingly evident that the way we view death determines, to a surprising degree, the way we live our lives."[1]

If you believe existence ceases with death, you might as well get all the gusto you can get in this life, since you only go around once.

If you believe in reincarnation, you won't be that worried about the here and now because you think you can keep going around again and again until you get it right.

If you believe hell is spent on earth while you're here, your behavior may not be influenced much.

But if you believe in the heaven and hell of the

Bible, you'll live your life in the light of heaven and tell your friends about the awfulness of hell.

Actually, if the Bible is correct, it won't matter what anybody thinks or how they believe. If the whole Christian deal is real, the opinions, philosophies, and religions of men and women won't amount to a hill of beans. Truth is all that will count. Whoever is right will win. Those who are wrong will lose big time. It makes considerable sense to figure out what's right. There's a lot on the line.

Sooner or later you will die. The Bible says that just happens once. "Man is destined to die once, and after that to face judgment" (Hebrews 9:27). Yet, we talked about five folks who died twice. How can that be?

God makes exceptions as He sees fit.

Why?

Because He's God.

But that might not be the reason in this case, because there are different kinds of death. Actually there are three. And if you are one kind of dead when you die, you'll spend forever dead.

Confused? Stay tuned. I'll explain in the next chapter.

Oh, I almost forgot.

I started this chapter with a story about Henry Bibby and never quite finished. I left you hanging with a vehicle chasing me down a narrow North Carolina back road at almost a hundred miles per hour. Well, the headlights turned off after about a five-minute chase. It ended up being no big deal. But I thought it would be more fun to wait until now to tell you.

Chapter Two

WHAT KIND OF DEAD ARE YOU? (If the whole deal is real, you don't have to be dead when you're dead.)

In chapter one we discussed our fear of death and its inevitability. We concluded that the odds of not dying made betting against it a very long shot indeed. In all of history that only happened to two guys, Enoch and Elijah.

But we only talked about death in one-dimensional terms. Death is really three dimensional: physical, spiritual, and eternal. Each is mentioned in the Bible where Jesus is speaking to a woman named Martha.

> I am the resurrection and the life; he who believes in Me shall live, even if he dies, and everyone who lives and believes in Me shall never die. Do you believe this? (John 11:25-26, NASB).

That's a tough passage, but look closely. You'll find three kinds of death wrapped up in the verse. Keep in mind that each kind of death has a corresponding life. Let me add some extra terms to show you what I mean:

> I am the resurrection and the life; He who believes [spiritual death to spiritual life] in Me

> shall live [eternal life instead of eternal death], even if he dies [physical life to physical death], and everyone who lives [who is physically alive] and believes in Me [spiritual death to spiritual life] shall never die [eternal life, not eternal death]. Do you believe this?

Death was not in God's original plan. It came with Adam and Eve's rebellion in all three forms: physical, spiritual, and eternal. Illness wasn't a part of the deal called life, either. But since the days after the Garden of Eden, bodies that weren't supposed to get sick, age, or die, have done so—making physical death a reality. People have been born spiritually dead ever since. And all those who don't solve their spiritual problem before physical death occurs are left in big trouble. They're in a pickle because what happens next is eternal death.

Each kind of death is different from the others, but all are interrelated. It's important to understand this interrelationship. If you're confused, relax. I'll explain in more depth. We'll start with physical death.

Physical Death

The first kind of death is physical death. The Bible says death occurs when your spirit, whatever it is and wherever it is, leaves your body (*see* James 2:26). When your conscious awareness, your soul—the entity or energy that is you—leaves the house you call your body, physical death occurs. What I am defining as physical death is different from the medical definition. Medical folks call you dead when your brain waves flatten out and your vital functions are irreversibly lost.

Has God made exceptions to His rules on death? Yes. He bypassed death for Enoch and Elijah—two men who never were destined to die. Are there other exceptions to God's general rule? I don't know. But remember, if there are exceptions, they are not the rule. The rule is: Man is destined to die once, and after that to face judgment. Women too, just like my mom.

My mother died a few years ago. I got a phone call one night. Most people get two calls like that in a lifetime. You know instantly, with very little being said. The reality is in the tone of voice on the other end of the phone. In this case the voice was a friend of my mother's third husband.

My mother had been an alcoholic. A few years before the end of her life, she lived in the skid row area down by the pier in Santa Monica, California. When she was in her mid-sixties, however, I had the incredible privilege of leading her to Christ. Her life changed dramatically and she lived several years relatively free from booze. She did start to stumble with her drinking again, and one morning the Lord laid her down on the sofa and took her home. It was as if God thought, *Oh, June, let's not do this drill again. I'll just bring you home and save us both a lot of grief.*

My stepdad wanted me to speak at her memorial service. That would be tough. I cry easily and fall apart at the drop of a hat. I couldn't, and wouldn't, say no to the opportunity; yet how in the world could I ever get through the service without coming apart? There would be people at the meeting who would never darken the door of a church. They had seen such great changes in my mom, and this would be a wonderful opportunity for me to share the message of Christ. I had to do it. But could I speak without coming unglued? I wasn't sure.

Grief passes with time, but not enough had passed. My emotions were tender. As I prepared the message, a memory would moisten my eyes. As I practiced giving the talk, a tender thought would bring tears. There was no way to get through the script without breaking down. I needed to be desensitized. But how?

I decided to go to the mortuary early. My stepdad wanted the body to be visible. Although I didn't like that much, it was his choice. I figured, *if I practice my talk for a couple of hours in front of my mom's body, I might be desensitized enough to get through the message in front of the attendees*. That may sound morbid, but I was desperate.

When I first saw her I was stunned. Although I recognized her, things just weren't right. Her mouth hung some because the muscle tension wasn't there, the makeup was wrong, and her hair wasn't combed the way she would have done it.

I started rehearsing my message in front of her body and the same things happened. I'd have a memory and start crying. I couldn't get past my natural response of grief.

For some reason I reached out and touched her hair. Then I touched her arm. I used my right index finger and was instantly sorry. She was so cold. I still remember the coldness on the tip of my finger. The top sixteenth of an inch of her skin was soft, but underneath it was like hard modeling clay. I recoiled, repulsed. That's when the Lord did me a big favor.

I didn't hear voices, but a peace came over me that said, "Jay, this is an old house and your mom ain't here. It's true that she used to live here, but she don't live here no more." It must have been an angel speaking because I'm sure the Lord would have used better grammar, but the message was clear. My mom was in heaven, and in a puff of smoke called my lifetime I would be with her. With that confirmation, whoosh! The tears went away.

I went into the prayer chapel for ten minutes and then went into the meeting and "greased" the message. I never balked or cried, not even once.

All of us will have to face physical death, both with those near and dear to us and personally. My mom died, my dad will, my wife, my kids, and their kids will also, and so will I. You will too. That's why a person ought to be ready.

It's true that death can sometimes be postponed. I try to stay in pretty good shape by working out five times a week. My heartbeat is in the mid-fifties. My blood pressure is 110 over 70. My cholesterol level is 176. I had a stress test and the doctor was impressed. We concluded that I am going to die healthier! I may put it off for a while, but I'm a dead man.

When physical death occurs you can't kill the energy or entity that is you. That just relocates to a place called eternity.

But where you spend eternity depends on whether you are still spiritually dead. What happens next to those who are physically dead is called the second death. One pastor I know says it this way, "The first death involves the separation of the body from the soul and spirit. The second death involves the separation of the person from God forever."[2] Let's see what that means.

Spiritual Death

The second kind of being dead is spiritual death. Surprisingly enough, you were born that way. It's part of the consequence of original sin. Adam's sin infected you through your dad. He got it from his father, and so on, all the way back to Adam. It's called a sin nature (some people call it the flesh), and everybody's got one, including my daughter. Grandpa found out about it early on.

My dad had retired to a house on Lake Pend Oreille in northern Idaho. We would go there during summer vacations. The fishing, boating, and water skiing were wonderful.

Work interfered with my going one summer, so Kim went to visit Grandpa, alone. She was a very mature, set-in-her-ways, five-year-old.

While there, Kimmy was demonstrating her stubborn streak and Grandpa sent her to her room until she shaped up. The instructions were, "Young lady, don't come out of that door until you are ready to act properly." He pointed to the door to her room.

The problem was that the closet for Kim's room doubled as a closet for the adjoining bedroom. If you crawled into the closet, hung a right and then a left, you would end up in the other bedroom. So that's what Kim did. Then she opened the door and walked into the living room with a pout on her face.

"I thought I told you not to come out of that door until you got rid of that look on your face," scowled Grandpa.

Pointing to the other door, Kim answered, "I didn't, Grandpa. I came out of that door."

Talk about walking a fine line! What is it that makes us want to stay on the edge—to push against the line? Why do we want to see how bad we can be?

Hey, did your folks have to teach you to be disobedient? No! You picked it up naturally. And that's the point.

Have you ever seen how little kids play with each

other? They're vicious. Shouts of "Gimmee!" and "Mine!" are accompanied with eye gouges and face scratching. The only time rug rats are sweet is when they're asleep. You see, they have a sin nature . . . and so do you. You were born separated from God. You were born in sin (*see* Psalm 51:5). You've got a sin nature and you got it from your dad (*see* Exodus 20:5). You need to face it—you were born spiritually dead.

The Bible says we're either children of God or children of the devil (*see* 1 John 3:10). Now, don't get upset. Cool your jets. If you aren't a Christian in the truest sense of the word, I didn't just call you a devil worshiper or a dirty, rotten person. Nor did I defame your character. That verse refers to ownership. Either God owns you or the devil does. It describes with whom you'll spend eternity. You are either spiritually alive or you're spiritually dead. Changing your status is your call. No one can do it for you, and it doesn't happen by being good.

Spiritual birth requires a decision. Spiritual deadness doesn't. As a matter of fact, failing to decide is considered a decision against God's solution and leaves a person spiritually dead. Unfortunately, "no call" is the decision most people will make. Matthew 7:13-14 confirms it. More people will choose hell than heaven:

> Enter through the narrow gate. For wide is the gate and broad is the road that leads to destruction, and *many* enter through it. But small is the gate and narrow the road that leads to life, and only a *few* find it (Matthew 7:13-14; emphasis mine).

You were born spiritually dead, separated from God, and at some point you became accountable for your sin. Although most people won't choose it, the Bible offers only one solution for your condition. It's called spiritual birth.

Spiritual birth occurs through Jesus Christ. Christ is the only way to solve the problem of spiritual deadness. He personally said so: "I am the way and the truth and the life. No one comes to the Father except through me" (John 14:6). God doesn't mention any other method. Jesus called it being born again. He spoke about it in John 3:

> In reply Jesus declared, "I tell you the truth, *no one can see the kingdom of God unless he is born again.*"
>
> "How can a man be born when he is old?" Nicodemus asked. "Surely he cannot enter a second time into his mother's womb to be born!"
>
> Jesus answered, "I tell you the truth, no one can enter the kingdom of God unless he is born of water and the Spirit. Flesh gives birth to flesh, but the Spirit gives birth to spirit. You should not be surprised at my saying, '*You must be born again*'" (John 3:3-7; emphasis mine).

We were born once physically. But according to Jesus, another birth is necessary, a spiritual one. It's crystal clear. The only solution to spiritual death is spiritual birth. And spiritual birth can take place only through Jesus Christ. God said so.

Physical death is unavoidable and ultimately out of your control. You can delay it some, but you won't escape it. Eternity is also unavoidable and out of your control. You will spend it someplace, like it or not. That is not true of being spiritually dead, however. You have the say-so in staying that way.

Here is an interesting thought. We make a big deal out of suicide, and I think we are correct to do so. Suicide should be against the law. Life is too precious to throw away. Yet, we don't make much of a fuss about folks who commit spiritual suicide. What does that say about our concept of the value of a soul?

Spiritual suicide is hearing the truth about Jesus Christ and not responding to it. People who reject the Son of God condemn themselves to hell. So don't wait too long to make your decision if you haven't already, because if physical death catches you spiritually dead, you're in the biggest trouble imaginable. You'll be a real hurtin' unit forever—because you'll have to endure eternal death—and that's what makes betting against the Bible so risky.

Eternal Death

Eternal death is final, absolute, nonreversible, and lasts forever. It is spent wherever, in whatever, hell is. (Hell will be discussed thoroughly in the next chapter. Right now we'll concentrate on eternity.)

Eternity is a difficult concept to illustrate, but here goes. Some have suggested a bird relocating every grain of sand on the earth, but that doesn't quite do it unless you never let him stop. Although there are a lot of grains of sand, there are only so many. Grains of sand are finite. So that illustration doesn't work.

How about getting on a plane going west and continuing until you're east? Sounds like a dog chasing his tail. You never would arrive. But you always would know how long you have been traveling because you would be aware of time.

Some people don't like that illustration because they see eternity as being without time. It may be that there will be no time in the new heaven and the new earth. God created time; He can eliminate it if He wants to.

God is the only One who can be anywhere and

everywhere at once. Not so with us. We're aware of time because we're confined. In eternity, although we will have new bodies, we probably still will be limited because of our restriction to them.[3]

It's interesting that time isn't a constant. Scientists have discovered that people in the mountains live longer than those at sea level. It seems that those closer to sources of gravity age faster than those further away. Therefore time goes slower in space than it does on earth. But there is another way to vary time as well, and the concept offers some interesting possibilities regarding eternity.

The theory of relativity makes time relative to motion. The faster we travel the more time is compressed. For example, traveling at 160,000 miles per second for ten years in space equals twenty years on earth. But 170,000 miles per second for a day equals twenty years on earth. Einstein postulates that at the speed of light (186,000 miles per second) all time exists in the present.[4] Maybe that's how God can say something like, "I never was, I never will be. I AM!" If in heaven all time exists in the present, we who go there will not be bound by time either. But I doubt that the same will be true in hell. Hell might be a place where time stands still.

Whew! That kind of thinking hurts my mind. Here's a thought about eternity that's more my speed. I was lighting my fireplace using a built-in gas starter, or "cheater." Having turned on the gas I held out a lighted match, but the gas jet blew out the flame. So, without turning off the gas, I fumbled around for another match, lit it, and thrust it into the opening. What do you think happened? Sure, a big "poooooof" made all the hair disappear from the back of my hand. All I had left were those curly, smelly little nubbins.

As I looked at the flames I thought about the times

I've passed my finger through a candle's flame. Almost everyone has done that. I decided I would do the same thing with the flame in the fireplace. Turning around to see if anyone was looking (I didn't want someone to see a grown man doing such a thing), I passed my hand quickly through the fire. It was so fun I did it a second time. Then I decided to put my hand in and leave it for ten seconds, just to see what would happen.

Stop what you're doing for a moment and look at a clock or a watch and count out ten seconds. (At least count one thousand one, one thousand two, and so on. Do it this time. You'll miss the whole point if you don't.)

Under most circumstances ten seconds goes by quickly, but in a fireplace it would be a long period of time, wouldn't it? I thought so too, so I didn't put my hand in.

What if you put your hand in and left it for a minute? That would be a long minute.

How about for an hour, and for some reason your hand wasn't consumed? Would it be a long hour? You bet!

How about a year, or a lifetime, or a really long time, like umpteen jillion, quadtrillion, nonillion, decillion, billion years? Now, that would be a long time in the fire.

Eternity is undoubtedly multidimensional, but since I'm an old athlete, and since old jocks aren't very smart, let's study eternity as a one-dimensional term. A line is one-dimensional, so that's what we'll use for our illustration.

Look to your left and imagine a clothesline running as far as your eye can see. If you're in a room, imagine the line running out through the wall. Have the line run right under your nose so that you have to look cross-eyed to see it. Now look to your right and see it going as far as your eye can see. To the left is eternity past, to the right is eternity future.

Let's plot some times on the eternal line. Using an

ultrafine-point accountant's pen, put a dot on the line right in front of your nose to represent ten seconds. Next, plot one minute. It's a dot too. An hour, a year, and a lifetime are also dots on the line. And get this, umpteen jillion, quadtrillion, nonillion, decillion, billion years is also no bigger than a dot. All the dots are the same size because the ultrafine-point pen is the only thing we have with which to mark. Actually, any whole number will appear as a dot because the line is so long.

Can you imagine umpteen jillion, quadtrillion, nonillion, decillion, billion years and have it only be a dot on a line that goes on forever? It's tough trying to grasp eternity because we're bound by our measurements of time.

Take one more step. Try to imagine spending forever, not with just your hand in a flame, but with your body totally immersed, experiencing the agony and yet never being consumed. That's the literal interpretation of what the Bible calls hell, and most people have a lot of trouble accepting that. If you are one of them, pay close attention to the next paragraph.

Keep in mind that illustrations never can depict completely the reality of what they are attempting to portray. A depiction is usually something less than the original. A copy of a video isn't as good as the original. It's true of a lithograph as well. Analogy works the same way. The real thing is better than a picture. Therefore, hell must be worse than any illustration we can dream up to describe it.

If the hell of the Bible is not literal fire, the real hell will be worse than our description of it.

Bingo! The Lord certainly got my attention with that revelation.

Mick Jagger, lead singer for the Rolling Stones, several times has referred to having made a deal with the devil. Mick gave his soul in exchange for all the world has to offer. I wonder how he will feel about the length of his lifetime after he gets to compare it with eternity? The former is a snap of the fingers. The latter is a timeless forever.

I'm trying to warn you about hell. My limitations as a writer keep me from doing a better job. And I don't know how to make you more aware of the true nature of eternity. I've tried. But heaven, hell, and forever are biblical concepts. Whether you end up in heaven or hell, you will remain there in a state of awareness forever.

I believe the whole deal is real. Since I value you, my part is to make sure you hear the truth. Your part is to respond. That makes the next move yours.

It's Your Turn

My wife, Mary, and I enjoy playing Uno with our son, John. Uno is a card game that requires placing cards on a stack. Sometimes a card played will require the rotation to change, or sometimes the next person in order will be skipped. The game moves quickly and is fast-paced. The players have to pay close attention.

We all play for different reasons. We're together to have fun, but conversation has to happen between hands. The nature of the game requires it. John and I are into competition. But Mary wants to visit and be social. It's easy not to recognize when it's your turn. We all lose our concentration occasionally, but frequently we have to remind Mary that it's her play.

After a while, John and I will make eye contact with each other and nonverbally agree to sit without saying anything, waiting for Mary to realize it's her play. She'll look up from her cards, see us looking at her, and say, "Oops! Is it my play?" After several times it gets pretty funny.

I don't want you to just sit there. You have a part in this deal. This book is intended as a reminder. I want you to respond with, "Oops!" and realize it's your play.

It's important, so let me remind you: You can't do much about physical death other than delay it. In light of eternity, delays in death are inconsequential. And you can't do anything about eternity. You are going to spend it . . . someplace. If the whole deal is real, you will continue on forever, regardless of your beliefs or decisions. But you do have the say-so regarding which place you'll go.

Where eternity is spent is a spiritual matter determined by your choice—not by how you've lived your life or how nice you've been. Spiritual birth is your decision. Do you want spiritual life or do you want to continue on spiritually dead?

Oops! Is it your turn? Have you made your choice?

You'll find some real nice people on both sides of the spiritual fence, and there are a whole bunch of nice folks sitting on it who refuse to choose. But be absolutely assured, there will be no fence sitters in heaven. No choice is a choice against Christ. When you die you go with the one who owns you and those on the fence do not belong to God.

If you let your sin nature run its course, you'll spend forever with the devil. And keep this in mind: satan[5] doesn't want to be with you; he just doesn't want you to be with God.

Someone said, "Man's greatest need is to know what is his greatest need." It is woman's, too. As the song goes, "The main thing in life is keepin' the main thing the main thing."

Being spiritually alive or spiritually dead at the time of physical death is the sole determiner of eternal life or eternal death.

The most important of life's decisions revolves around spiritual life and spiritual death.

Life poses no situation that has graver consequences. No dilemma you'll ever face rivals this one. And being nice has absolutely nothing to do with the outcome.

Oops! Is it still your turn? Place your bet.

Eternity hangs in the balance of your choice and your forever will be spent in either hell or heaven. We'll talk about both places in the next two chapters.

Chapter Three
WHERE TO NEXT—HELL? (If the whole deal is real, most folks choose hell.)

My friend, Dave Sundquist, flew into the arms of God in a plane crash some years ago. He was ready when he died.

During his B.C. (before Christ) days, Dave lived in Las Vegas. He had developed a system for forecasting the point spreads on football games that really worked. So well, in fact, that the Mafia wanted him to join them and reveal his formula. He refused, so they put a hit out on him. Dave started running.

Somewhere in the Dakotas, as a way to pass the time, he started reading a Gideon Bible he had stolen from a motel room. He began in Genesis and the further he read, the more he saw God's holiness and the more he became convinced of his sin. It got so bad that one night in a motel room, he crawled under a chrome and formica dinette set, covered it with a blanket to make everything as dark as he could, got into a fetal position, and rocked and screamed. He later confided that the only reason he didn't commit suicide was that he was thoroughly convinced the result would be worse than his current condition.

My friend did not believe death would free him from despair. He believed it would make it worse—beyond anything he could imagine. Dave believed he would go to hell, but didn't know what to do because he hadn't read far enough.

To make a long story short, Dave kept reading his Bible, got to the New Testament, and read about what Jesus Christ had done for him. There was no one to explain the concepts, but Dave kept reading and led himself to the Lord. He asked Christ to represent him to God and committed himself to following Jesus. Dave was a gambling expert. He bet his eternal soul on God being right.

Did that keep him from dying? Nope! It happened when his plane hit a mountain. I got to speak at his funeral.

Dave Sundquist was iron in my life. The Bible says, "As iron sharpens iron, so one man sharpens another" (Proverbs 27:17). I titled my message, "Some of My Iron Is Gone." His death was a tremendous personal loss for me. And yes, I cried some as I spoke. But not nearly as much as I did a few minutes later.

Dave had a pretty good voice and had recorded some of his music on homemade audiocassettes. One song he sang was "It Is Well With My Soul." At the end of the service they played it. Dave was singing at his own funeral telling us that things were great. We felt sorry for ourselves and grieved, but Dave was just fine. If the whole deal is real, he had found eternal peace in heaven and said so as he sang. His soul couldn't be any better and it would be that way forever.

Dave understood eternity before he faced it. Perhaps

understood is too strong a word; let's say he was ready for it. Not everyone is. Least of all, those who deny God.

Only Atheists Deny Eternity

The concept of eternity is native to every society ever studied. Only those who stifle the still, small voice of God and deny His existence don't recognize a forever somewhere. But regardless of the mental gymnastics exercised by the ones who deny God, when they stand before Him they will be without excuse (*see* Romans 1:20), because God has planted the awareness of Himself in the hearts of all people.

It still amazes me how those who reject the reality of their heavenly Father cry out, "Oh my God" or, "God help me" when they are surprised, scared, or in deep weeds. When it gets down to brass tacks, they tend to cut through all the fluff and rhetoric. That's when most atheists admit their awareness of God.

It's interesting that when Gorbachev, an atheist, was being arrested by the perpetrators of the failed coup in August, 1991, he didn't tell them to go to Siberia; he told them to go to hell. Tell me, is Gorbachev really an atheist?

The rest of humanity is aware of God, although it's true that some do nothing more than acknowledge Him and love themselves. But even with inappropriate worship, intuitively most of us are aware that we continue on after we leave our earthly house. That eternity is a universal concept in societies around the world is one of the proofs of its reality.

You are intuitively aware of eternity, so proving it is probably no big deal to you. You don't have to be persuaded about its existence. You understand that the odds on eternity being real are pretty good. But where you spend it ought to get your interest. The Bible makes us aware of our need for concern.

Is the Bible God's revealed word to mankind? Yes or no? Which do you believe?

If you're not sure the Bible is for real, make sure you keep reading this book, clear through chapter eleven. There will be enough stories and laughs to get you that far. You'll also have enough data to make a logical decision by then.

If you believe the Bible, it is impossible to read the book without realizing that eternity is spent in one of two places—heaven or hell. No other possibilities are offered. No other options exist.

Assuming you believe the Bible, are you aware that the basic theme of the Old Testament is the promised coming of a Savior and that the New Testament is about the fulfillment of that promise through Jesus Christ? Since Christ is the central focus of the Christian faith, you'd think that what He had to say was very important, wouldn't you? It is!

Try this on for size. Jesus said more about hell than He did about love, and He spoke of hell more than all the rest of the biblical preachers combined. Hell occupied His subject matter two-thirds more than heaven did. Hell is real, my friend. Jesus said so—and it's the ultimate in scary thoughts.

Are you thinking, *Jay, are you trying to scare me?*

My answer is, "You bet!"

It'll Scare the Heaven into You

Going into a battle during Operation Desert Storm, an officer hollered to his troops, "Give 'em hell!"

I'm hollering in this book, "Give 'em heaven!" Through the working of the Holy Spirit of God, I'd like to scare the heaven into you—and the hell right out.

Does the use of fear as a motivator bother you? Is the use of terror as a method to get your attention upsetting? Here's what one psychologist says about its use:

> When fear is used to motivate people, especially sensitive children, in the name of God, it is a grave mistake and constitutes one of the biggest dangers and difficult obstacles that young people have to overcome in order to live happy, fruitful, adult Christian lives.[6]

That's one side of the coin. Here is the other:

> If men do not fear the terror of the Lord they must experience that terror. **If you are not afraid of hell, you are almost certainly going there** (emphasis mine).[7]
>
> Why, then, do so many vehemently oppose frightening children? They don't. They scare children away from fire, from electric sockets, from poisonous drinks or pills, from snakes, from certain toys, from anything that threatens them.
>
> Why, then, do almost all seem to oppose frightening children with hell? The answer is obvious: they wrongly fancy that children are not in danger of hell. **Can you imagine that a mother who would give her own life to save her child's wouldn't do everything to save her child from hell if she knew there was any danger?** (emphasis mine).[8]
>
> Why scare preaching? Two reasons: (1) God, in His Word, is a Scare Preacher; (2) The fear of hell is the only thing most likely to get worldly people thinking about the kingdom of God. **No**

> **rational human being can be convinced that he is in imminent danger of everlasting torment and do nothing about it. But, you say, there are many now who fear hell, or say they do, and yet don't believe or seek the gift of faith. That is true, but, as we say, that only proves that they are no longer "rational human beings"** (emphasis mine).[9]

There is no question that some over zealous preachers have done an overkill on hellfire and brimstone. But the "turn or burn, flip or fry, change your stroke or go down in smoke" kind of preaching has become a thing of the past.

Is there a place for fear preaching? I think so. The Bible makes it clear that fear is a legitimate reason for coming to Christ. Granted, it is not the most desirable, virtuous, or noble of reasons. But it is a reason. Jesus made that clear:

> I tell you, my friends, do not be afraid of those who kill the body and after that can do no more. But I will show you whom you should fear: Fear him who, after the killing of the body, has power to throw you into hell. Yes, I tell you, fear him (Luke 12:4-5).

Jesus also preached rewards. Heaven later. And love, joy, peace, and all the rest of the fruit of the Spirit can be enjoyed now. Although it seems selfish, what I can get out of a right relationship with Christ is a legitimate reason for considering Him. Whether it is a better reason than fear, I'm not prepared to say. I think so, but I'm not sure.

Of course, the most noble of reasons and the purest is the response of a grateful heart. When we understand what Christ did for us by taking the sins of mankind on

His shoulders, our response should be gratitude and worship. When we put together the price (Christ's death) and the payoff (overcoming the justice of hell and spending forever with God), can we respond any way other than with thankfulness?

All three reasons are biblically sound, regardless of the psychologist's warning. Perhaps Christ's use of fear and rewards are ways to get our attention. And then, once having gotten it, He processes us to the stage of gratefulness. Maybe the order ought to be reversed. Maybe we first ought to tell people about the love of God. If that doesn't work, then tell them what they can get out of a walk with Christ. If that doesn't do it, then, if they'll listen, resort to scaring the hell out of them, and replace it with the heaven that comes through a right relationship with Jesus Christ.

I don't know for sure. But this I do know:

> *Jesus Christ used fear as a way to communicate the seriousness of the issue of hell.*

I'm afraid. In my book *Something's Fishy*, I develop the truth stated in Matthew 7:13-23. The facts are: 1) most people will choose hell over heaven; and 2) far more folks in the church are going to hell than I ever dreamed possible. Those are two frightening conclusions. Are you afraid of hell? If you're not right in Christ, you should be.

Funny thing about fear. We hate it. That's why we tend to deny those things that cause us to be afraid. And interestingly enough, when it comes to hell, most people are in a state of denial.

It's Hard to Believe

The *c* word. "You have cancer," is the doctor's final pronouncement. It hits like a ton of bricks. It's one of the most dreaded combinations of letters in our language. Classically, the reality of having cancer is denied for days, and sometimes even weeks. We don't want to hear what we don't want to hear.

"This is officer Smith with the state highway patrol. I'm very sorry to have to tell you this, but your son was in an automobile accident and was killed." It's too painful. Our first response is *there must be some mistake*. The reality of the loss is oftentimes not faced until the funeral. Some refuse to deal with it for months or years.

John Gerstner has an interesting insight into classic denial. He gets to the heart of the matter in a hurry:

> Most people who are going to hell find it more comfortable to deny that fact than admit it. Yet denying hell is one of the main reasons they are going there. God can't lie Himself, and can't stand the company of liars.
>
> Their enemies assure them that they are not going to hell. Their friends warn them that they are. Foolishly, they make their enemies friends for telling them lies. They make their friends enemies for telling them the truth, though with the kind of friends they have, they need no enemies.[10]

Consider me a friend. I want you to know about hell. If someone gave you this book, consider him or her a friend, too. Your friend cared enough about your soul to risk the relationship, just so you'll know. It takes a lot of love to do that. The uncaring thing to do would be to let you go to hell without risking anything of themselves.

What if your house was on fire in the middle of the night and your neighbor woke up, saw it, but went back to sleep without telling you? How would you feel toward him? Close? Hardly!

"But I feared waking you. You might have been mad and it would have hurt our relationship." If that's the depth of his commitment, you don't have much of a relationship, do you?

Some neighbors would do more. They would call the fire department. But the best ones would kick down the door or break a window to get in. They would risk their lives to make sure you were safe. Now, that's the kind of people I'd like to live next to. How about you?

Is your spiritual house burning? The person who gave you this book cares enough to risk the friendship to tell you. Cherish a relationship that has the depth of this one. Rejoice greatly. This one is a good friend indeed!

Is your spiritual house on fire? Acknowledging that is sometimes difficult. Remember the emperor who had no clothes? He walked about stark naked while everyone complimented him on his wardrobe. Think of what could have happened to the one who passed by and said, "Hey emp, did you know that you're buck naked?"

"I can't be, everyone said I look great."

"Trust me; you're making a fool of yourself. Go home and look in the mirror."

Does the emperor cut off the man's head or look in the mirror? Do you ruin the relationship with your friend or look in the mirror (the Bible)? If you are a rational person, you will look. Let me tell you what you'll see. If you're honest, you may see a person going to hell—but your tendency will be to deny it and get mad at your friend.

Sticking Your Head in the Sand

George Gallup, Jr. has compiled a variety of data in his fascinating book *The People's Religion: American Faith in the 90s*.[11] So have Patterson and Kim in their tacky 1991 release.[12] I've summarized their findings:

- 94% of the American population believes in God
- 81% believe in judgment day
- 81% of the religiously active believe in life after death
- 50% of the nonreligiously active believe in life after death
- 32% of the nonreligiously active do not believe in life after death
- 66% believe in heaven
- 46% expect to spend eternity in heaven
- 53% believe in hell
- 4% expect to spend eternity in hell

Only four percent of the American population believes they are going to hell. That is the most staggering statistic of all. For two reasons: 1) that so few see it as a real risk to be dealt with; and 2) that even four percent would be content to go there without doing something about it.

Why the dramatic differences between heaven and hell?

Denial!

Billy Graham, in his book on death, concluded, "Gallup surmises, and I tend to agree, that some of the reasons why more people believe in heaven than in hell is that "hell is like death—people try not to think about it."[13]

That's bizarre. It's the ultimate in supernatural ostrich syndrome. Both concepts (heaven and hell) come from the same source (the Bible), but we mortals buy into one while denying the other, thinking belief will change reality. It's not rational, but it's the way most people deal with hell.

Denial, when coupled with our natural compassion and fear, produce a hope that hell will be something less than the Bible says it will be. We can't understand how a loving God could allow such a place, so we develop concepts like purgatory (going to a hell-like place for a period of time, depending on how bad you've been), and paying penance (it's hard to believe that Christ paid our entire debt on the cross, so we tend to think that more must be done, and we should be the ones to do it). Our conclusion is that if hell is for real, only really bad people go there (like in the movie *Ghost*, where one of two nice people who are living together is murdered. The murderers went to hell. The fornicator who lived with his girlfriend went to heaven).

If there is a hell, some folks would agree that murderers ought to go there, along with child molesters and drug pushers. But there is a large group who believe that everyone ends up in heaven.

Everybody Goes to Heaven

Some of the most subtle forms of denial show up in doctrine that waters down the Bible. It's an attempt to get everyone into heaven and everybody out of hell.

Some believe that hell is spent on earth and we all go to heaven. Or if there is a purgatory, we all end up in paradise in the end after we have paid penance. These ideas are called universalism, but there is no biblical support for the concept. The Scriptures have to be twisted to make them even suggest the possibility.

Universalism is a nonbiblical way for people to cope with their fear of hell. It is an escapist philosophy. Pure denial. So don't get sucked in. Mental gymnastics don't alter biblical truth, not if the whole deal is real. Not everybody will end up in heaven. As a matter of fact, if the whole deal is real, most won't. Jesus said so at the end of the Sermon on the Mount.

Despite what Jesus said, most people believe that hell is not a forever kind of place. They prefer to believe in the concept of annihilation.

Nobody Goes to Hell

There are some high-powered theologians[14] who subscribe to the hope that those who go to hell simply end as an entity. It's called annihilation. Eternal punishment is not a part of this idea. An individual has no awareness or existence. The person just ceases to be.

Consider this thought as an answer to annihilation:

> Justice demands adequate punishment. Since punishment itself never produces repentance, justice requires it to go on forever. Even the very expression, "the annihilation of the wicked," is an outrage against justice, because sin requires punishment, not non-punishment which non-existence certainly is.[15]

Hell is real and it doesn't end. It can't because the same Greek and Hebrew words that describe the length of heaven are used to describe the length of hell. The wording of the Bible demands that one place last as long as the other, and that people in one location remain just as aware for just as long as those in the other. Take just one example, from Matthew 25:46:

> Then they will go away to eternal punishment, but the righteous to eternal life.

Since heaven will last forever, those who go there

will enjoy it eternally. The same also has to be true of hell, only it's not enjoyed. Those who go to hell will suffer forever because that's how long it lasts. The Bible cannot be manipulated around that absolute fact.

The Word of God says the smoke of hell will go up forever and ever. Revelation 14:11 states, "And the smoke of their torment rises for ever and ever." Mark 9:43 says hell is a place "where the fire never goes out." The fires of hell are fueled by the justice of God; that's why they never go out.

> *Hell is a beginning, not an end. It is the beginning of an eternal state of torment. It is not the end of existence.*

Denial Doesn't Change Reality

Billy Graham, the great evangelist, had this to say about why people deny hell:

> Certainly war, hunger, terrorism, greed, and hatred are hell on earth, but, except for the Bible believer, a future hell became part of the ash heap of ancient history. As hell was becoming for many no more than a swear word, sin was also an accepted way of life. People began to look to science, education, and social and moral programs as possible solutions to the growing chaos of an insane world. If people can ignore what the Bible calls sin, then they can quite logically discount what it says about the reality of hell.[16]

We refuse to spoil the present over concern for the future. But then when the future becomes the present, we're always sorry we didn't exercise our foresight.

Prepare for your future. Planning for retirement in

your later years is wise, but paying little attention to the inevitability of your encounter with timelessness is foolish indeed. A lifetime is but a few short years. Eternity is forever. Don't let it be the ants and the grasshopper story all over again. The ants prepared for winter while the grasshopper fiddled. Don't be a grasshopper. Don't fiddle around with hell. You're playing some long odds if you don't believe that place is to be avoided at all costs.

With so much at stake, playing ostrich and sticking your head in the sand doesn't seem very bright. Ignoring reality doesn't change it. The odds on the Bible being wrong are too remote. We'll talk about why in the last chapter. No document has been more scrutinized over a longer period of time and stood the test any better. Its truth defies the odds makers. But we shouldn't be surprised. After all, God wrote it.

It is not my intent to do an exhaustive study on hell. I just want to let you know that nice people go there and to give you some idea of what's in store for those who do go. With that in mind, here are a few glimpses of that awful place called hell. Its descriptions are enough to make your skin crawl.

Glimpses of Hell

Some people think hell is going to be like being on the sun. The gravitational pull would make it hard to move around, and it's so large they'd probably never come into contact with anybody else. If they did, it would be two people with their sin nature, turned totally loose, so they'd be at each other's throats the whole time. They never could leave because of the gravity and they'd have the torment of the heat of the sun, and yet somehow wouldn't be consumed.

I doubt if the sun illustration is possible because the Bible says hell will be outer darkness. So, whatever kind of fire hell will have, it won't be the kind we know because there won't be any light. Unless, of course, hell exists at the base of the flame.

There is a place at the base of a flame that is invisible—the place where fuel is changed from a solid to gas or vapor is colorless. We see it only because of reflected light. At that point there is no light. It is an absolutely dark space. Could that be what hell is like—that place in a flame where there is the total absence of any kind of light?

Since God will be the only source of light in eternity and hell is a place where God isn't—then hell is a place where there will be no light. By definition, darkness is the absence of light. That makes hell a place of utter, absolute darkness.

Have you ever been in an underground cave? So deep that there was no light at all? The guide warns you, then turns out his light. You wait for your eyes to get used to inky blackness, but nothing happens. There is no adjustment to be made. There is no light. Part of hell will be the absolute absence of light for eternity, coupled with a conscious awareness of the pain produced by fire. Imagine—absolute aloneness, total darkness, and unending agony.

Here's an unknown writer's opinion of hell:

> There's no way to describe hell. Nothing on earth can compare with it. No living person has any real idea of it. No mad man in wildest flights of insanity ever beheld its horror. No man in delirium ever pictured a place so utterly terrible as this. No nightmare racing across some fevered mind ever produced a terror to match even the mildest hell.

> No murder scene with splashed blood and oozing wounds ever suggested a revulsion that could touch the borderlands of hell. Let the most gifted writer exhaust his skill in describing this roaring cavern of unending flame and he would not even brush in fancy the nearest edge of hell.

The commentators I read collectively agree: Hell will be a place where there will be no righteousness, it will be a dimension that's absolutely and eternally separated from God, and it will be an abode of constant judgment and retribution. The word *hell* connotes doom, hopelessness, and futility.

Hell is both a place and a condition. One writer phrased it this way:

> Life apart from God is existence filled with guilt, hollowness, despair, meaninglessness, and helplessness. The agony of eternal punishment apparently involves both body and soul because Scripture says both are ultimately cast into hell. Apparently this would involve inner anguish as well as detrimental effects upon the body. It may involve the torment of being cut off from fellowship with one's fellow man, and also the results of living within a society of men from which the grace of God has been completely withdrawn.[17]

Chafer says of hell, "No more decisive terms could be employed than those which describe men as being without Christ, without promise, without God, and without hope."[18] But you ought to know that no one is in hell right now. The dead who don't know Christ aren't there yet. They're in Sheol-Hades.

Sheol-Hades

In the Old Testament there is a place called Sheol. In the New Testament it's called Hades. It's the same place; the words are basically synonyms. Some writers call it Sheol-Hades.

During Old Testament times, everybody who died—both the righteous and the unrighteous—went to Hades. But there were two levels, the penthouse and the basement.[19] The penthouse was like heaven and was a nice place to go. The basement was like hell, not as bad perhaps, but it was a terrible place to be.

The righteous Old Testament saints, like Abraham, who believed God and were counted as righteous, went to the penthouse. The unrighteous went to the basement. One commentator wrote, "It appears from this passage [Luke 16:19-31] that Hades is composed of three compartments: 'Abraham's bosom,' 'the great gulf fixed,' and 'the place of torment.'"[20] The heaven-like place is called Abraham's bosom and is separated from the place of torment by a chasm.

Christ died, and during His three-day period in the grave went to both Hades and paradise. He went to Hades and took all those in the penthouse to a place of paradise called heaven, the place Christ had prepared for them, the place where God lives.

Tim LaHaye agrees with this scenario:

> We know that the Lord Jesus went to paradise, for in Luke 23:43 He told the thief on the Cross who cried out for salvation, 'Today you will be with Me in Paradise.' So we know that Jesus went directly from the Cross into the paradise section of Sheol-Hades. Now look at Ephesians 4:8-10. This passage reveals that paradise is no

> longer located in Hades, but was taken by Christ up into heaven. This would indicate that the believer now goes to heaven, where he is joined with the Old and New Testament departed saints, leaving the former paradise section of Hades an empty compartment.[21]

Since that time, those who die knowing Christ, who are spiritually alive, don't go to Hades. They go to heaven. Jesus left those who were in the basement. They will end up in hell—but not for awhile. Several events have to unfold before that happens. I'll talk more about that in a minute.

By the way, nobody has a body in either heaven or Hades. Everyone exists in spirit form only. But those in heaven get their new bodies before those who are in the basement.

Spiritual Bodies

Both those in heaven and Hades are there in an intermediate, bodiless, spirit state. This state is both conscious and immediate upon death.

As I studied this material I began asking why the ancient patriarchs didn't go straight to heaven. I liked this answer best:

> You are probably wondering why the Old Testament saints were directed to the place of comfort or paradise in the first place. After all, they believed in God while they lived. The answer is found in the inadequacy of the covering of their sins. In the Old Testament, sins were temporarily covered by the blood of a "lamb without blemish or without spot." But an animal's blood was not sufficient to permanently cleanse their sins (*see* Hebrews 9:9-10). Sacrifice was an

exercise of obedience, showing their faith that God would someday provide permanent cleansing from sin through the sacrifice of His Son.

When our Lord cried from the Cross, "It is finished," He meant that the final sacrifice for man's sin was paid. God in human flesh could accomplish what no animal sacrifice could ever do—atone for the sins of the whole world. After releasing His soul, Jesus descended into Hades and led all the Old Testament believers, held captive until sin was finally atoned for, up into heaven, where they are presently with Him.[22]

Since the time Jesus emptied the penthouse, all people who are dead spiritually when they die physically go to Hades, the basement . . . that's all that's left. The penthouse has been moved to heaven. But as I said, we only go as "soulish" or spirit. We don't have bodies in either place. Not yet, anyhow.

Then, when history ends, at the end of the age, a series of final events will take place. Some seem bizarre, but it's also bizarre that Christ is looking forward to spending eternity with you and me. So, don't get hung up in the unusual nature of things. Remember, what seems strange to us doesn't matter at all if the whole deal is real. Our ways are not God's ways. If it is real, you can't pick and choose. Folks can argue about some of the little things that aren't clear, but the significant events in the Bible are too well documented to dispute. Those in the know generally agree on the following end-times events (scholars do argue about the sequence):

1. The rapture (the taking of Christians out of this world, when the dead in Christ get their spiritual bodies).

2. The tribulation (three-and-a-half years of good times on earth followed by three-and-a-half years that will be the worst in history).
3. Armageddon (the final battle at the end of the tribulation).
4. The coming of Christ (ending the battle that would have destroyed the populations of the earth).
5. The Millennium (a thousand years of peace on earth under the reign of Christ). The beast and the false prophet (who are satan's henchmen during the tribulation) are the first to be thrown into hell (the lake of fire) at the beginning of the period. Satan is bound and sent to a pit for a thousand years with his demons.
6. At the end of the Millennium, satan will be turned loose for a short time to test the faith of those born during the thousand-year period.
7. The Great White Throne judgment (the spirits of the dead in Hades will be united with their respective eternal, new bodies and will be judged along with those alive at the end of the millennium).
8. The casting of the unrighteous into hell. Satan is first (remember, the beast and the prophet are already there), then his demon followers, and then the unrighteous.

Items one and seven in the above list mention getting new bodies. Those in heaven will get a new body similar to the one Jesus had after the resurrection. He walked through walls; enjoyed eating; was touched; flitted between heaven, the upper levels of Hades, and earth; and had a body like the one Peter, James, and John saw at the transfiguration:

> There he was transfigured before them. His face shone like the sun, and his clothes became as white as the light (Matthew 17:2).

Whatever kind of body Jesus had at that event is the kind of body we'll get at the time of rapture. The new bodies of those who physically died (and were spiritually alive in Christ) will be united with their spirit first. Then those Christians who are alive at the time of the rapture will get their new bodies as well. We'll talk more about that in the next chapter.

Some people believe that those in hell will exist in a disembodied state, and that such an existence will be one of the greatest judgments of all. I don't think that's the case. If it were, then those who are in heaven, who are in a disembodied state awating the rapture, would not be at peace. Since the Bible says they are content in the presence of God, without their bodies, then hell must be something more.

I believe those in Hades will get their new bodies at the time of final judgment at the Great White Throne:

> The sea gave up the dead that were in it, and death and Hades gave up the dead that were in them, and each person was judged according to what he had done (Revelation 20:13).

Although the passage doesn't specifically say so, it looks like the bodies of the dead (from the sea and the grave—the Greek meaning of the word *death*) are joined with their respective spirit (from Hades) and together face judgment.

Dead bodies are scattered about the earth and the sea in various states of decomposition and dissolution. The God who made 'em in the first place is the same God who can put 'em back together in a changed state.

If body and spirit are joined, each person will have a different kind of body than when he was physically alive. This body is the hellbound counterpart of an anatomy like Christ's resurrected body, except this new body will experience and withstand the torment of hell, and along with its spirit will endure eternal punishment. It's a kinda' double-whammy retribution reunion, lasting forever. We're talkin' bad berries . . . but it will be even worse for the devil.

What about Ol' Sloughfoot?

Satan, who was locked in a pit for a thousand years at the beginning of the Millennium, will be let loose for a short season to flush out those who were born during the Millennium and hated living under Christ's authority. Then the devil will be cast into a lake of fire, hell—the place God created for him in the first place.

Satan will be preceded into this final fire by his two tribulation-period henchmen. When Jesus Christ returns, both the beast and the false prophet will be thrown into hell. They appear to be the first to go in. Satan will follow a thousand years later.

There appear to be levels of punishment in hell (*see* Mark 12:40; Luke 12:47-48; 20:47; John 19:11). The Bible suggests punishment according to works on this earth. The deepest part of the pit is reserved for the devil himself. The beast, the false prophet, and the demonic host will apparently be at another level. People will then be positioned according to their works at the upper levels of hell. The concept of degrees of punishment is consistent with the parallel concept of rewards in heaven, so it's a likely scenario.

I was speaking to a group of junior highers at Hume

Lake Christian Camp in California a few years ago. We were outside around the fire circle and I was doing my heaven-and-hell talk. I told about the levels of hell, how satan would go in first and deepest, and how the demons would go in next. It was then that some kid in the back row yelled out, "And then the Celtics."

Being a former L.A. Laker, and having been beaten by the Boston Celtics in the seventh game of the NBA championships by one basket, the thought made me smile. We even burst out laughing. But I wouldn't wish hell on them, although some of them will end up there, along with a bunch of the Lakers and the rest of the players in the league who don't decide to follow Jesus Christ.

By the way, don't make the mistake of thinking satan is going to rule in hell. He won't be sitting on a throne holding his scepter laughing at the plight of others. Hell was created for his torment. All those who agree with his philosophy will join him, but hell wasn't created for them; it was created for the devil. But he'll not rule there. Satan will be in torment and all those with him will be in torment as well.

If the Bible is right, Cindy Lauper is wrong. Cindy said she could hardly wait to go to hell, because that's where all her friends would be and they would be able to party forever. Wise up, Cindy—there will be no party in the lake of fire. The screams you'll hear will not be "party hardy" sounds.

A Good Look at a Bad Place

In Luke 16 we get a glimpse of what Hades is like. We can make some assumptions about hell from our observations. I call it the story of the rich man and Larry.

> There was a rich man who was dressed in purple and fine linen and lived in luxury every day. At his gate was laid a beggar named Lazarus, covered with sores and longing to eat what fell from the rich man's table. Even the dogs came and licked his sores (Luke 16:19-21).

There was a rich kid who dressed well. Clean! Slick! Very together. GQ, look out! Whatever is hot right now is what he had plenty of. He also lived it up daily. In other words, he was a total party animal. They called him Sweet William the Third.

Bill had it all. Electrostatic rock monitor speakers with a bass booster in the corners of his room. The best CD and DAT recorder, along with all the finest audio equipment. A forty-two inch tube TV with Surround Sound. And a well-stocked refrigerator right next to his bed. Our moneyed man-about-town drove a new Corvette with a super-amped sound system. Of course, he was great looking and was one of those unusual teenagers who didn't have any zits. Our affluent athlete was a standout jock; the star quarterback on the football team, high scorer on the basketball team, the top track guy, and hit .600 for the baseball team. The luscious lover was great in the girl department, got straight A's without studying, and was student body president. What can I say? The guy was a stallion, Sir Studly, a Mister Everything for sure.

The son of the gardener was named Larry. He lived by the entry to the estate in the gatekeeper's cottage down below the rich kid's house. Larry had a pretty tough life. He had some terrible zits and was covered with sores. We're not just talking simple pimples here. Larry had acne vulgarus. His was a severe case.

To make matters worse, Larry had to eat the rich kid's garbage. And to top it off, the poor guy didn't get paid enough to afford a doctor. The medical plan for Larry was obviously deficient, because instead of a prescription for his face or some medicine like Oxy 10, they got a dog to lick his zits. (See verse 21: "Even the dogs were coming and licking his sores.") How gross! Poor Larry. (Remember, I didn't write this stuff. You'll have to take this one up with God.)

> The time came when the beggar died and the angels carried him to Abraham's side. The rich man also died and was buried. In hell, where he was in torment, he looked up and saw Abraham far away, with Lazarus by his side. So he called to him, "Father Abraham, have pity on me and send Lazarus to dip the tip of his finger in water and cool my tongue, because I am in agony in this fire" (Luke 16:22-24).

It came about that this poor, pitiful, and pathetic person died and went to heaven. I think the doctor diagnosed Larry's cause of death as a case of infected zits.

The very next day Dollar Bill was driving his 'vette, wrapped it around a tree, was killed, and went to Hades. Looking up, the rich kid saw Larry in the penthouse.

The first thing we learn about Hades, and probably about hell, is that the rich kid knows what's going on in the penthouse.

Those who go to hell will probably know what they missed out on in heaven . . . forever.

As to how that happens in utter darkness, I don't have a clue. But if Hades is like hell, it looks like the residents will always be aware of the cost of dying spiritually dead. They will always be aware of what they missed.

The second observation comes when the rich kid hollers out a demand to the penthouse, "Send Larry down here to comfort me."

Can you believe it? He's still trying to boss Larry around. This pompous, once-opulent juvenile still has his personality intact, but all the good parts have been removed. Only the negative elements remain.

Can you imagine spending forever with a bunch of people who have their unrestrained sin natures turned loose? Me neither. Or even worse, how about enduring eternity alone and isolated with only your rottenness to contemplate?

Then our money-bags moppet says, "Have Larry touch my tongue with a drop of water; I'm in agony in this flame." Notice—he is suffering. There is flame, and he is in the middle of it.

Pain and anguish are characteristics of hell.

> But Abraham replied, "Son, remember that in your lifetime you received your good things, while Lazarus received bad things, but now he is comforted here and you are in agony. And besides all this, between us and you a great chasm has been fixed, so that those who want to go from here to you cannot, nor can anyone cross over from there to us" (Luke 16:25-26).

The fourth point of the passage is the great chasm that exists between heaven and hell.

Once you're in hell, you are there forever.

The gap can never be crossed. Never! Either way.

This passage of Scripture eliminates the possibility of any kind of purgatory. You can't run a few of your laps in hell then get out. There is no serving penance and cutting out for the promised land. No sir! The canyon can't be crossed.

> He answered, "Then I beg you, father, send Lazarus to my father's house, for I have five brothers. Let him warn them, so that they will not also come to this place of torment."
>
> Abraham replied, "They have Moses and the Prophets; let them listen to them."
>
> "No, father Abraham," he said, "but if someone from the dead goes to them, they will repent."
>
> He said to him, "If they do not listen to Moses and the Prophets, they will not be convinced even if someone rises from the dead" (Luke 16:27-31).

When Richey Rich understood the eternal nature of his fate, he begged the guardian of heaven to tell his five brothers about the reality of hell so they wouldn't have to go there.

The gatekeeper reminded him, "We've told them already; we gave them the Bible. They wouldn't read it."

The kid said, "No, do something spectacular, like bringing somebody back from the dead. Then my brothers will believe."

"We did that too," the gatekeeper responded. Jesus has already raised several people from the dead. That didn't work—you still didn't believe Him. They haven't either. Like you, your brothers will have no excuse."

The rich kid was burning. There was no escape. He

had made his decision while physically alive but found no opportunity to change it in eternity. "He had sunk to a death beyond prayer, a condemnation beyond forgiveness, and a doom beyond the reach of Christ."[23]

Assuming Hades is hell-like, the story of the rich man and Larry gives us a few peeks into what hell probably will be like. To get a more complete picture, I looked up the verses about hell and reduced them to words and phrases that summarize the biblical picture. The list follows:

1. You'll keep your personality with your sin nature turned loose
2. Satisfaction is never available; there is never any fulfillment
3. An absence of all that's good
4. In the presence of all that's bad and evil
5. Unrestrained demonstration of selfish urges
6. Continual burning
7. Consuming fire
8. Unquenchable fire
9. Eternal destruction
10. Outer darkness
11. Weeping and gnashing of teeth
12. No presence of God
13. No glory of God's power
14. Lake of fire
15. Burns with brimstone and fire
16. Second death
17. Extreme anguish
18. Worse than death itself
19. Degrees of punishment
20. Wrath and fury
21. Tribulation
22. Distress

23. Sudden destruction
24. No escape
25. Pits of nether gloom
26. Torment goes up forever and ever
27. You'll have no rest
28. You'll know what's going on in heaven and be aware of what you're missing forever

That's a thumbnail impression of hell. Pretty grim, huh? And yet some people think life on this earth is more important than their existence afterward. Hell is a terrible price to pay for such distorted values. It's an awful consequence for making just one bad bet. Are you gambling that you're right and God is wrong? If so, you're trying to be God and you go to hell for that.

Stay out of hell. You don't want to go there. It's the pits—literally. The other option is much better—heaven! All those who die in Christ (spiritually alive at the time of physical death) will go there. We'll take a look at the place Jesus called paradise in the next chapter.

Chapter Four

WHERE TO NEXT—HEAVEN? (If the whole deal is real, only a few people go to heaven.)

Here is an article written by a college student who will miss heaven unless he has a change of heart. A friend in the ministry sent me this campus newspaper clipping after hearing about the writing of this book. The column is a pretty good presentation of the condition of most of the folks in America:

> God is coming back, and I'm scared.
>
> A recent poll published in *U.S. News and World Report* says that 78 percent of the people in the United States believe in Heaven, while 60 percent of the population believes in Hell. These are both up from 1981 totals, which were 71 percent and 53 percent, respectively.
>
> Actually, that didn't bother me much. Just because people believe in heaven or hell doesn't mean they necessarily believe in a particular religion. I mean, I'd like to think that there is heaven, even though I am not affiliated in any way.
>
> What did bother me was the subsequent letters

to the editor. Those saying that everybody that didn't embrace the gospel of Jesus Christ and accept Him as their personal Savior were on the Amtrak to hell.

Of course, these are much the same people who are lying out in front of abortion clinics telling women that they can't control their own bodies. They are similar to the people who have determined for us that certain books shouldn't be read because they are "ungodly."

And of course, they are related to the infamous Spanish Inquisition, where "heathens" were killed for refusing to convert to Christianity.

Now, despite what it may sound like, I don't hate Christians, nor anyone of any other religion. What they worship is their business, not mine. I may not agree with them, but I support their right to believe in what they choose.

Unfortunately, it seems this is a one-way street, and this annoys me. Since I am a religious "free agent," I'm targeted as a potential convert. In trying to convert me, I am being told that what I believe, no matter what it is, is wrong.

Anyone who has ever walked in front of the UCen [University Center] during the day can identify with what I'm saying. Crossing the area between Storke Plaza and the UCen, one has to run a gauntlet of people handing out flyers advertising Bible Study. Here you see more blank stares than in an upper-division economics class. As people walk past, the outstretched hands with little flyers wave while passersby refuse to meet the gaze of the saved. Go out there and watch sometime, it's really funny.

But the gist of it isn't funny, it's frightening. The people out there don't know me. They don't know my beliefs. They only think to spread the gospel, whether I want to listen or not.

Now, I've long known that if there is a Heaven that goes by the rules commonly stated by Christians, then I am on my way downstairs the moment I die. I don't consider myself a heathen, I've never killed anyone, and I don't think I've committed any major sins, but according to the rules, I'm outta' there. Express elevator to the subbasement.

But I don't really care. I have my own beliefs, and nothing has ever been shown to me that has caused me to change them. I believe in a "higher power"—not necessarily the Western concept of God, but a force that created the galaxy and everything in it. Whether it is "God" or a process of nature is a matter of debate. However, it is something immensely more powerful than mankind, and therefore deserves some respect. I'd also like to believe that there is some kind of eternal reward, where good and just people go after death. However, I don't believe in any concrete thing.

And if God exists, then I find it hard to believe that He is so vain and self-centered that He requires every entity in the universe to worship Him constantly. He knows that I am grateful for existence, and that I am grateful for the opportunity to live and grow. He also knows that I get angry over things that have occurred and say things that I later regret. But since He created me, He knows that this is simply the way I am. He also knows that I don't feel that it is necessary

> to travel to a place of worship once every seven days to tell Him specifically that, "Yes, God, I do still love you and would like to dearly thank you and tell you for the millionth time that you're really, really great."
>
> But perhaps that is the way He is. Perhaps He needs people to tell Him how wonderful He is. Perhaps my thanking the Fates and being happy about life isn't enough. Perhaps He is an entity that requires constant worship. Perhaps the only people who attain heaven are those who subjugate themselves to His will.
>
> But if that is the way Heaven is, then I don't want to go there.[24]

The writer knows there is a God, but he doesn't know God. The result: he's scared. And it is well that he should be.

He assumes that since so many people believe in heaven and hell, the places must be real and he hopes the masses are right. He's not concerned about hell. But he can't stand the idea of there being only one way to heaven. Funny! This guy is not alone in that reaction. The "one-way reality" chafes us all. We have friends and loved ones whom we want to have in heaven with us. That's why it's so hard to believe nice people really do go to hell.

He doesn't like the limitation of his choices. Restrictions are an infringement on his freedoms, and he doesn't like it one bit. He dislikes Christ—or anybody representing Him—for saying there is only one way to heaven. He wants to be like Frank Sinatra. He wants to do it "his way."

Not unexpectedly, his next beef is the curse of

hypocrites in the church. How many are there who use them as their reason for denying God? Christianity would be great if it weren't for Christians. But I like what a friend says when somebody lays this line on him: "Yes, there are hypocrites in the church. But there's always room for one more."

Having vented his anger, the writer lets us know he dislikes what Christians stand for, but his feelings are not personal—he dislikes what they do and how they do it, not them. He especially hates impersonalized witnessing.

But he may have misread the situation. If the "spreader of the gospel" saw the writer's value as an individual and was motivated by concern for his soul, then he should have been flattered and his response should have been, "Thank you for your concern." But the writer felt them looking at him as if he were a pig or a piece of raw meat, and he is offended.

The writer sees himself as a good guy, and if that's not good enough, then so be it. He concludes that if the whole deal is real, he is going to hell. *Christians must be wrong*, he thinks. Nice people don't really go to hell . . . or do they? He's not sure.

He doesn't understand much about God. He's clueless as to His character. The writer incorrectly assumes that whatever God is to you, that is the way He is. And if God is not the way the writer thinks He ought to be, then the young man really doesn't care to know Him.

The writer incorrectly thinks God needs our praise. He doesn't realize that praise will be a natural outflow. Our heavenly Father is so incredible, we'll need to praise Him. Worship will be a get to, not a have to. If we couldn't worship, we would bust our buttons trying to hold it in.

The young man who wrote this article reflects the

thoughts of so many I've talked to over the years. He wants to go to heaven only on his terms, not God's; and if being nice isn't good enough, then so be it!

His last two sentences say it all. If he has to subjugate himself to God, he doesn't want to go to heaven. The bottom line is: He'll go anyplace, including hell, rather than bow down. If heaven is a place where you have to bow down, then he'll pass.

That says it all.

It is the nature of the beast to fight the mandates of God—it's our sin nature showing itself, and it's why we go to hell.

Two armies of the world that have taken the strongest position against God have been Hitler's troops and the forces of the one-time U.S.S.R. Both marched using the goose step. The head is tilted forward, bowing the neck. The knees are straight and stiff. What a statement demonstrating the condition of the heart.

That's the writer's problem too, isn't it? He just covered it up with a smoke screen of words and arguments. He would rather miss heaven than bow down. Without a change of heart, miss it he will. Let's take a look at what he'll miss.

Paul's Peek into Heaven

Three people have seen heaven—Jesus Christ, John in Revelation, and Paul. Jesus made it. John saw it in a vision. Paul probably went there and came back. We're going to study Paul's account of heaven just like we studied the rich man's account of Hades.

Paul saw heaven after he'd been stoned. (That's the New Testament version of the word, not the current interpretation. It referred to rocks, not drugs or booze.)

There were three kinds of stoning in Paul's day. The

first was a legal or judicial type. Officials built a scaffold eight to ten feet high. Accusers would throw the accused off and try to drop a large rock on his chest or head. Then everybody would stand around in a circle and throw rocks.

The second manner of rock throwing was called "pit stoning." It was the primary method of enforcing capital punishment. The pit was eight to ten feet deep and fifteen to twenty feet across. Accusers would throw the accused in and everybody would encircle the hole and throw rocks until the dude was dead.

The third way was a plain-old-lynch-mob kind of stoning. The mob would make a circle around the accused and chuck rocks at him until he was dead. People didn't like this method very much because if someone sidearmed a rock, and really hucked it hard but missed, somebody on the other side of the circle would end up getting hit.

You can understand why the folks preferred the pit stoning method as the capital punishment of choice. It was safer for everyone—except the accused. And it was cheaper than having to build a scaffold. Paul preferred it, too. He held everyone's coats while Stephen was stoned. There was a time when he loved seeing those Christians get rocked. But what goes around, comes around. The apostle probably didn't notice who was grasping the garments when he got his. It was the pits. The story comes from Acts 14:8-20.

Paul, Barnabas, Titus, and company had been chased out of Antioch and Iconium, so they hiked the twenty or so miles to Lystra. Taking a lesson from Jesus and Peter, they found the most noticeable crippled man they could find. When you heal one of those guys they have a tendency to leap up and run and jump and praise God all over the place. It never fails to draw a crowd. So that's what Paul did, and sure enough, the healed hobbler drew a crowd.

But Paul hadn't boned up on his local history and wasn't prepared for what happened. Tradition had it that the Greek gods Zeus and Hermes had come to town generations earlier and apparently only one family had shown them the proper courtesy. So the gods snuffed all the townspeople except the household who showed them a good time. It left such an impression that the folks who resettled Lystra built a church and actually staffed it with a priest, just in case the gods ever returned.

So when Paul and Barnabas did their thing with the lame guy, the people thought Zeus and Hermes had come back. Not wanting to mess up twice in a row, they tried to worship the traveling band of miracle workers. It was a natural mistake. Barnabas was tall and statuesque, like Zeus. And Paul certainly had a special command of the language, just like Hermes, the god of oratory. Archeology has confirmed the existence of the temple dedicated to the gods, and a plaque commemorating their return shows a date which corresponds with the time the apostles would have been there.[25] We don't know who the original "gods" were, but the story is true. Archaeology has confirmed it.

As Paul and Barnabas were negotiating with the townsfolk as to where they ought to direct their worship, troublemakers from Antioch and Iconium arrived. The folks at Lystra changed their tune in a hurry. Peer pressure oftentimes does that.

How quickly they forget. How fleeting is glory. Heroes one minute, targets the next. The same thing happened to Jesus and it's about to happen to Paul. As a future warning, it will happen to anyone else who takes a stand for Christ, you included. They'll love you one minute and hate you the next. That's the way it is for those who follow Him. There will be persecution for the believer.

Paul's stoning probably went something like this (remember, this is pure conjecture on my part, something straight out of First Carty and Second Hesitations, but it will make the account more interesting): The mob moves in on Paul. The others undoubtedly get roughed up in the process, but the mob centers their attention on Paul because he's the talker.

The people probably beat Paul for a while then threw him into a pit. Falling on the rocks strewn in the bottom of the pit from previous stonings, Paul gets cut up and bruised badly. People surround the rim and begin throwing. The apostle scrambles to his feet.

Paul is holding his hands up to protect his head. He doesn't see the two-hander coming at him. The boulder strikes him on the lower part of his leg, shattering it, crushing his foot, causing the apostle to fall to his knees.

That's when another big, heavy, two-hander comes at him. Paul tries to dodge, but he can't move. The rock catches him in the chest, dislocates his shoulder, breaks his clavicle, and knocks the wind out of him. The blow drives him to the ground.

Now he's on his side gasping for air, lying on the only hand he can move. The other is useless. He has no protection for his head. And here comes another big one. There is nothing he can do so he watches it all the way in. The rock hits him in the eye and crushes the side of his skull. They kept throwing rocks until the body was just barely visible, but Paul didn't know it. He was probably dead. But that's not the end of the story.

Afterward, the delegated officials climbed into the

pit, pulled Paul out from under the rocks, pronounced him dead, hoisted him out of the pit, dragged him out of town, and left him for the dogs to eat. That's the way it was done.

Victims of pit stonings were either dead or not far from it. Those who survived were hardly capable of travel. Weeks or months of rest and rehabilitation would be required to put a person back on his feet.

But the Bible says that while his disciples stood around him, Paul got up, walked back into the city, checked things out, and the next day started a sixty-mile trip with Barnabas to Derbe. In other words, God worked a miracle and healed Paul while his followers watched.

It must have been like a fast-forward scene in a movie. The wolfman losing his fangs and hair and becoming human as we watch the screen. Cinderella at the stroke of midnight returning to what she was before her fairy godmother waved the wand. The flower closing in a time-lapse nature film. As the disciples watched, the cuts healed, the broken bones mended, and the bruises went from red, to blue, to yellow, to healed. It was a miracle. And God fixed it all—well, almost all.

Fourteen years later, Paul wrote about what happened next. He saw heaven:

> I know a man in Christ who fourteen years ago—whether in the body I do not know, or out of the body I do not know, God knows—such a man was caught up to the third heaven. And I know how such a man—whether in the body or apart from the body I do not know, God knows—was caught up into Paradise, and heard inexpressible words, which a man is not permitted

> to speak. . . . And because of the surpassing greatness of the revelations, for this reason, to keep me from exalting myself, there was given me a thorn in the flesh, a messenger of Satan to buffet me—to keep me from exalting myself! (2 Corinthians 12:2-4,7, NASB).

He's not sure if he died or not. He probably did, but he's not sure. Paul says, "I know a man in Christ [me] who fourteen years ago, whether in the body or out of the body [man, I don't know if I was alive or dead!], God knows. Such a man [me] was caught up in the third heaven."

(Biblically, the sky above is regarded as the first heaven; the planets, stars, and the universe beyond is the second heaven; and the place beyond, where God dwells, is the third.)

Paul ends up saying that he was caught up into paradise (heaven) and heard and saw some things that were so fantastic that he was forbidden to tell anybody about them. And just to remind him not to tell, God gave him a thorn in the flesh.

Here's a wild guess as to what that thorn was. We know Paul had some kind of an eye problem. It's possible that God healed everything except where the rock smacked him in the head. And the reason He didn't heal the eye is because what Paul saw was so incredible that when he came back, if he were able to articulate all he had seen, people would want to commit suicide so they could get to heaven faster than planned and circumvent God's plans for them on this earth. Paul was great with words. So if anyone was capable of painting convincing word pictures of heaven, it was Paul.

Regardless of how it came about, I'm convinced God

left Paul with a thorn in the flesh to remind him not to tell all that he saw. Why? For our benefit. Heaven is that wonderful.

> *God gave us enough information to cause us to look forward to heaven, but not enough to cause us to forget those around us who aren't going.*

Although there are two-thirds more verses on hell than there are on heaven, God still has much to say about paradise. There are five hundred and fifty references to it. Here are a few more glimpses.

Heaven

During the four hundred years of silence between the writing of the last book of the Old Testament and the first book of the New Testament, some of the words for God and heaven became synonyms. The New Testament word for heaven often means God. Sinning against heaven means sinning against God. Often the kingdom of Heaven means the same as the kingdom of God. The Bible tells us heaven is filled with God, so being in heaven will put us in the actual presence of God. Heaven is continually being with God. It goes beyond the perfection of the Garden of Eden because we'll be with God all the time—not just when He comes to visit. We'll always be visiting because we'll live there. What an incredible thought!

In addition to God being there, everything that ought to be important to us is there, including our Savior, name, inheritance, reward, treasure, and citizenship. Fellow believers from both Old and New Testament times will be there. And the angels of God are there as well.

The Bible calls heaven a place. How many light years is it to heaven? Who knows? Is it even in this dimension? I couldn't tell you. The Bible does say heaven is up. Paul was caught up, Jesus ascended and descended, and numerous verses refer to heaven as up. I don't know if that's a general statement or if it's specific. If up is literal, consider this: if no matter where you stand on earth heaven is up, then the third heaven must surround the second heaven. Remember, the Jews called the sky the first heaven, the planets and stars the second heaven, and the place where God dwells the third heaven.

Some scientists believe the universe is spherical. If heaven is literally up, the expanse that exists beyond wherever the second heaven ends (planets, stars, galaxies, and so on) is where the third heaven begins (where God lives). John MacArthur says, "Heaven encircles our universe and is as big as our God."[26] That makes God very big indeed. I don't know if that's where heaven is or not, but it's fun to think about.

Heaven does appear to be a long way away. Or is it? Jesus said to the thief on the cross next to him, "Today you shall be with me in Paradise." They would make the journey in a hurry. Today! They must have a heavenly warp drive. "Beam me up, Scotty" is a favorite term from "Star Trek" (although it was actually never spoken on the program). The transporter in the *Enterprise* took apart a person's molecules in one place and reassembled them in another. It sounds like the angels might have a heavenly transporter, doesn't it? Those are wild thoughts, but there are more.

The Bible says we are predestined to be conformed to the image of God's Son, so when we're in heaven we will have bodies like the one Jesus had (*see* Romans 8:29). Just like Jesus did with the thief, He will enable us to flit around heaven and the heavens at will. Sounds fun to me!

What kind of body did Jesus have? He ate, but didn't have to. It looks like He did it because He liked to eat. Chowing down is a satisfying experience. So He ate.

In Oregon, local strawberries are available for only a few weeks. We have to import our strawberries from Texas, California, and Mexico at other times of the year. I love strawberries, but we can't afford the out-of-state berries. Besides, the local berries are better. So Mary always buys two big boxes of local berries when they are ripe, and I try to eat them before they spoil. In other words, I try to O.D. on strawberries to get a fix that will last me the rest of the year. I love the challenge, and I love strawberries. But let's face it; I also love to eat.

Traveling around the country on speaking engagements makes for lots of eating out. When I'm invited to a home for dinner, folks always cook their specialty. It's not unusual for me to gain five pounds from Saturday to Wednesday. I have to work out pretty hard between trips to maintain my weight.

Imagine eating whatever, whenever, just for the taste of it—but it won't have to be Diet Coke. What a fun idea. I'm looking forward to heaven. Not just for the food of course, but won't that be a fun part? Imagine doing your shopping on the planets of the universe and eating the produce of the galaxies. Sounds great to me!

In addition to eating, Jesus appeared suddenly, walked through walls, could be touched, flew, talked, and was transfigured (His body was brilliant like the sun). His body was also perfect. No physical impairments (except for the wounds in His side and His hands and feet, which He kept for our benefit). No aches or pains. No parts wearing out. No sore lower back, no stiff neck. And we'll get one just like it.

We weren't designed to be disembodied spirits. We are terrestrial creatures. We need a bod, so God made us soul and body. Those of us who die in Christ prior to the rapture will be separated from our body until that time of reunion. Then God will put the bodies of the saved dead back together in a glorified form and unite them with their respective spirit. When my spirit comes together with my new bod, if I have a choice, after thanking God, I'm going to eat some strawberries. And then I'm going to dunk a basketball, from the waist. I've always wanted to do that.

The Bible tells us there will be a new heaven and a new earth. And the capital city of the new heaven will be a new Jerusalem. Since this is not a book on heaven, I'll leave that detail for your further study. Just be aware that we'll need bodies so we can walk around town when we don't want to fly. A resurrected body is part of the experience of heaven. Wow! What a deal.

Heavenly Summary

But wait, there's more.

It's something like a television commercial. If you buy the widget, you'll get a chingadeer at no extra cost. And if you order right now, they will throw in a whatchamacallit. There's a whole lot more to heaven than flying around in a new body, eating everything in sight.

John MacArthur described heaven on one of his tapes as follows:

> Heaven will be perfect freedom from all evil forever. Never a sinful thought. Never a selfish

thought. Never an evil word. Never a useless word. Never an evil deed. Never defiled. Never unclean. Never imperfect. Always doing everything which is perfect and holy. No doubts, no fear of God's displeasure. No temptation. No persecution. No abuse. No division. No discord. No disharmony. No disunity. No hate. No cruelty. No fights. No disagreements. No disappointments. No anger. No effort. No prayer (there will be nothing to pray for). No fasting (there will be nothing to fast for). No repentance (there will be nothing to repent of). No confession (there won't be any sin). No weeping (there will be nothing to make you sad). No watchfulness (there will be no danger). No trials. No teaching, no preaching, no learning (we'll have all spiritual understanding and there will be nothing to learn). No evangelism or witnessing. Perfect pleasure. Perfect knowledge. Perfect comfort. We will love as Jesus loved, absolutely and perfectly. And we will have perfect, complete, unending joy.

In heaven we'll never have to apologize, we'll never have to confess, we'll never feel bad. We'll never have to make any corrections, never have to clarify, never have to explain what we really meant, and we'll never have to straighten anything out from confusion because nothing will ever be confused. We won't have to fix anything, repair anything, adjust anything, or replace anything because nothing will ever wear out or malfunction. Never have to help anybody, nobody will need help. Won't have to deal with satan, demons, or sinners. Won't have to defend ourselves, there will be no attack. We'll never cry, never be alone, never be lonely, never be hurt emotionally or physically. We will never have to be cured, counseled, coddled or entertained. We'll always be filled with joy. Never have to do anything special for anybody because everything we do will be special to everyone all the time. There will never be any grief. We'll never lose anything, never miss anyone, and we won't have to be careful because we won't ever make a mistake. We won't have to plan for contingencies or emergencies, because there will never be a Plan B. We'll never have to avoid danger because there will be no danger.

Heaven is the experience of eternal perfection of body and soul.[27]

But wait! There is still more. I did the same thing with the verses on heaven as I did with the verses on hell. The following is a summary of what God wants us to know about where He lives:

1. The place where God dwells
2. A place of righteousness
3. We can worship God there (by the way, if you don't like to do that now you might find you won't have the opportunity to do so later)
4. No hunger
5. No thirst
6. No tears
7. No death
8. No sadness
9. No pain
10. No hard labor
11. Always be with the Lord

12. Paradise
13. Beautiful
14. Magnificent
15. Nothing unclean
16. God will be our light
17. Lots of places to dwell (it took God six days to make this world; Christ has been working on heaven for almost two thousand years. It should be nice)
18. No sex (I have a friend who said, "Man, if there's no sex in heaven, I don't want to go." My physical relationship with my wife is fantastic, but if everything in heaven is better than that, let's go. Heaven must be great.)
19. New and perfect bodies
20. Every spiritual blessing is ours
21. Physical descriptions of heaven speak of all the things that are the ultimate in beauty to us (gold, silver, crystal, precious jewels)
22. Retain our present personality, with the sin nature (flesh) removed
23. No age (Somehow every person will be distinctive, just as they are now, except they will not appear young or old)
24. We'll be served by the angels
25. We'll be served by Christ (the most staggering conclusion of all)
26. Not limited by time
27. In charge of many things
28. In heaven we're going to worship, reign, and serve proportionate to what we have done here on this earth with the time, talent, and treasure we've been given

29. In heaven we'll do all the good things we do here, only we'll do them perfectly. The things that we enjoy here we'll have the opportunity to do there in a perfect state

Go back to pages 74-75 and contrast the characteristics of hell with those of heaven. There's quite a difference, isn't there?

Life's a Taste

My son did his undergraduate studies at the University of California at Berkeley. It's a wild and bizarre place. I saw a bumper sticker on an old car there I don't think I'll ever forget: Life's hard and then you die. Have a nice day.

Life has its ups and downs—but is very difficult for some. So when I tell you that the Bible says our life on this earth is just a foretaste of life in heaven, you might be less than thrilled. If your life has been hard, that may not be good news. If it's been real tough, you may not have even had a taste of heaven yet.

Stop reading for a few moments and think of some of your most pleasurable moments. Make it the best of your spiritual experiences. Take a stroll in your mind and recall some of the special times.

The great things in life are love, joy, peace, patience, kindness, goodness, faithfulness, gentleness, and self-control. These experiences reflect the fruit of a godly walk. They are the qualities of life we experience when we yield to the leading of God.

Consider the depth of love you have experienced. In heaven it will be far deeper than you've ever imagined because you will never be let down by someone who loves you.

Think of the most joyous moment in your life. It wasn't even close to the joy you'll experience in heaven because it wasn't perfect. It was mixed with the sadness and sorrow and worry life produces.

When was the last time you were really at peace? You've just skimmed the surface of the peace that awaits. The noise of the world was disturbing you.

Do the same with each of the remaining words: patience, kindness, goodness, faithfulness, gentleness, and self-control. Consider your experience with them. Heaven will take you permanently deeper in each, and will keep you there forever. Remember, your most wonderful experiences in this life are both a foretaste and a promise of something better in heaven. That's a big-time concept and it blows my imagination off the scale.

My grade-school-age son came forward at a meeting where I was speaking to make a significant decision in his life. What a moment. My daughter has chosen to serve God on the mission field. Words can't convey my joy at her decision. My wife and I led a friend to Christ. He had been on my prayer list for over twenty years. The fulfillment of the moment still lingers. Those are but tastes of common occurrences in heaven.

Have you ever played with a puppy? Prayed with a friend? Had a belly laugh so hard that you gasped for air and had to wipe tears from your eyes? That's run-of-the-mill stuff in heaven.

Drive from Banff to Jasper in Alberta, Canada. Every turn of the road offers a new vista. It's unparalleled beauty. Take a look at the Oregon coast from Newport to Florence. There's nothing like it. Tour Yosemite Valley or backpack in the High Sierra. Fly over the Alps. Are you getting the idea? As magnificent as the scenery is, it's commonplace in heaven. Those places don't hold a candle to what is waiting for us in the place where God dwells.

It's Inconceivable

Where would you like to spend forever?

That sounds like a dumb question, doesn't it? Who in his right mind would choose hell over heaven? Yet the Bible tells us that most will make that very choice. I'm reminded of the buzz word from the movie *Princess Bride*—inconceivable. But I know why. Most do not believe that nice people really do go to hell. The majority of people do not believe that the whole deal is real.

Is it real? Consider this: "Every shred of evidence for the resurrection of Christ is evidence for eternal life in heaven."[28] If Jesus Christ conquered death, then there is a heaven. All that Easter stands for is proof of heaven. And the Holy Spirit is a pledge, a payment of earnest money (*see* Ephesians 1:13-14). Consider Him an engagement ring, the promise of the glories of heaven to come. What great thoughts! But it won't mean much if all we do is think about it. We need to live in the light of heaven.

Looking toward heaven is an evidence of salvation because we have a heart that is set on God and we want to commune with Him. We should be making life's decisions with our eyes on heaven. And we need to make sure our friends understand what they run the risk of missing.

I don't know where you are spiritually as you read. I don't know if you are an on-fire, goin'-for-it, no-holds-barred, Jesus-lovin' believer; if you are lukewarm; or if you are cold to the things of God. If you're on fire, perhaps this book will encourage your passion for those who run the risk of missing heaven. If you are lukewarm, my prayer is that these words will be energized by the power of God to fire you up. If you are cold, let me pose a question.

The Diagnostic Question

If you were what we call dead and were standing before the gates of heaven as a voice boomed out saying, "By what right do you desire to enter My heaven?" what would you say?

Perhaps your response would be, "Uhhhhhhh, I was a good person. I was born in the United States and I never murdered anybody."

"A good person?" the voice might say. "Compared to whom?"

Timidly, you might respond after stammering and stuttering, "Hitler."

"Yes, you compare well to Hitler, but how do you compare to Christ? He is the standard. You must either be as good as Jesus or have His recommendation to get into this place. I know you aren't as good as He is, so will He stand up for you? Have you stood up for Him? Do you know Him? Are you a friend of My son?"

Actually, you won't have a thing to say. Romans 3:19-20 says you'll be silent in your sins. You'll know that an all-knowing God is totally aware of your sin and that there will be no snowing Him. You can't snow God—and you'll realize it.

At a time like that, you won't need a lawyer. You'll already have been pronounced guilty. What you'll need is someone to pay your fine.

There is good news. Someone did.

Jesus asked Peter, "Who do you say that I am?" Peter had the right answer. "You are the Christ," he said. "My Savior" is what he meant.

Jesus is asking you the same question right now. Is His inquiry falling on deaf, passive, busy, or willing ears? How you heard the question will determine who you are going to bet on—you, Jesus, or some other person.

As a kid I remember my mom cleaning my ears with a wash rag. An adult finger wrapped in a washcloth will not fit inside a little kid's ear. Why do parents repeatedly insist on trying to stuff that combination of items in there? No wonder I used to scream and kick. She would say, "You could grow potatoes in here."

You probably don't have dirt in your ears anymore, but your ears are like dirt. So is your heart.

There are four ways to hear, just as there are four heart responses to the Word of God. These four classifications have a lot in common with four kinds of dirt. You'll "dig" what I'm talking about in the next chapter. How you hear will determine your response to the question, Who do you say that He is?

Chapter Five

WHICH PLACE? THERE ARE CLUES IN YOUR CLODS

(If the whole deal is real, you can tell where you're going by your dirt.)

Dirt is an interesting commodity. It's a real supply-and-demand item.

I was involved in building a mobile-home park some years ago. It was necessary to move a lot of dirt. When we finished making our cuts, leveling, and providing necessary drainage, we must have had a trillion yards of the stuff. Our pile was almost a block long, thirty yards wide, and forty feet high. There was no other construction going on around us and no one needed fill dirt, so we couldn't sell it. Relocating the stuff would cost a fortune, even if we had a place to put it. So we held on, hoping the nearby freeway construction would begin before the city required us to move the pile.

The dirt sat there for a year and the deadline for removal was drawing near. But the freeway construction did begin and they were desperate for clean fill dirt. Also, they hadn't checked with the city and didn't know how badly we needed the pile removed.

They needed clean fill dirt. The dirt they needed

couldn't be dirty. It had to compact to meet code, so purity was a crucial factor. It couldn't contain big rocks, debris, biodegradable material, or hunks of concrete. Our dirt met their standards and we cut a deal, making a nice profit. Clean dirt has great value when somebody wants it. Dirty dirt is not worth a thing.

Remember, we are just dirt. God made us from the soil. The result is that most everything we touch gets dirty. Look at what we're doing to our environment.

How can some people believe that man is basically good? It's beyond me. Wars, aggression, selfishness, violence, and destruction are all characteristics of humanity. Our sin has made us dirty. The term *dirt* fits us nicely.

Since we are all dirt, how is it that some dirt goes to heaven, while the rest goes to hell? How clean does clean dirt have to be? I know some real nice clods. Does nice dirt really go to hell?

Actually, there are four kinds of ground. Let's see if we can figure out which ones are clean enough for heaven:

> A farmer went out to sow his seed. As he was scattering the seed, some fell along the path, and the birds came and ate it up. Some fell on rocky places, where it did not have much soil. It sprang up quickly, because the soil was shallow. But when the sun came up, the plants were scorched, and they withered because they had no root. Other seed fell among thorns, which grew up and choked the plants. Still other seed fell on good soil, where it produced a crop—a hundred, sixty or thirty times what was sown. He who has ears, let him hear (Matthew 13:3-9).

That passage tells us we are one of four kinds of dirt: 1) hard, useless ground at the road's edge; 2) rocky, shallow soil; 3) ground covered with weeds, thistles, and thorns; or 4) fertile and productive soil. After reading this chapter you should end up identifying with one of them. Most Christians (80 percent)[29] identify with third soil.

Scholars continue to argue with one another as to which soils are heaven bound and which end up in hell. Theologians are supposed to do that. It's part of what they do. Some say that second, third, and fourth ground are all going to heaven. Others are convinced that only fourth soil will go. The argument has been intense of late. I think all of #4 soil and some of #3 go to heaven. I wrote my second book, *Something's Fishy*,[30] just to throw my two cents into the debate.

Few (if any) serious Bible-thumpin' scholars give much of a chance to first soil. Only raging liberals, new agers, universalists, and the hopeful "I'm a good person" kind of people do that. Virtually all agree that fourth soil will be stored in heaven. The debate primarily centers on second and third ground. But let's talk about all four anyhow.

Dirt #1

When I am speaking on the four soils, I pull out a sack, reach in, and start pulling out stuff. The first item is a cassette tape. It represents a tape of Christian elevator music. I say represents, because I told the person who wanted to give it to me that I didn't like Christian elevator music and he should give it to someone who appreciates it. In other words, I rejected the tape my friend offered me.

People do that with Christianity. When the message of what Jesus Christ did for us is presented, some people overtly and immediately reject it.

But there are other ways to reject. Dipping into my sack again, I pull out a marking pen designed for underlining passages of Scripture. A friend gave it to me. The price tag is still on it—$1.95. But I don't like it much. It's poorly designed. It's hard to pull the cap off, I can never tell if it's right-side up or not, and the clip is uncomfortable against my thumb. Now, I'm not going to find my friend and say, "Here, I don't want your stinking marking pen." That would be rude. So I'm going to take it to the store and get a buck ninety-five for it.

Some people accept the gift of Christian hospitality and its accompanying lifestyle as a good way to live and raise a family. They are interested in what they can get out of it, not what they can put into a relationship with Christ. They may look like Christians, but really they have rejected the gift. They prefer the benefits but don't want the affiliation.

Reaching into the sack the third time, I pull out the most awful, gaudy, extra-wide, paisley tie you have ever seen in your life. I call it "a tie only a mother-in-law could give." Frankly, it looks like the veins in my legs. The tie hangs in my closet growing an ever deepening line of dust across the top where it hangs on the tie rack. I'd get rid of the thing if I could (Goodwill won't take it), but my mother-in-law always checks my closet during her visits to make sure it's still there. So I have to keep it.

(For the record, my mother-in-law didn't give the tie to me and she doesn't do any of the things I say she does in the story. She's great and I love her to bits and pieces. But being an exhorter, I'll do anything to make a point. Besides, I have her permission.)

Children have to live with the faith of their Christian parents, and they often hang it in their closets until they head off to college or leave the house to start their own lives. That's when they either put it on, pack it up (and find it some years later), or throw it away (which is the case more often than not). Hanging it in the closet, never intending to wear it, is a form of rejection.

These are just three of many possible ways a person can reject Jesus Christ. Matthew 13 continues and explains what happens to those who choose to reject:

> Listen then to what the parable of the sower means: When anyone hears the message about the kingdom and does not understand it, the evil one comes and snatches away what was sown in his heart. This is the seed sown along the path (Matthew 13:18-19).

In the first soil the devil plays a part in the rejection process. (Birds, like those in verse 19, are often biblical portrayals of satanic activity.) But regardless of what the evil one does, each person is responsible for his or her own decision. The bottom line remains: those represented by the first dirt remain dirty in their sins. They rejected the Son of God, and if physical death catches them before they change their minds about Christ, they will go to hell.

Hell as the destination for the Dirt #1 is confirmed by a parallel passage from Luke 8:12: "Those along the path are the ones who hear, and then the devil comes and takes away the word from their hearts, so that they may not believe and be saved."

That's it. It's official. First dirt is not saved and is on its way to hell. So, if you are betting that people in the first soil are going to heaven, you are betting against the Bible.

If the whole deal is real, regardless of how nice a person is, if he is represented by first soil, he is going to hell.

People in first soil run the gamut of morality and philanthropy, from Hitler to Albert Schweitzer. But being a good person is not a way out of Dirt #1. One must believe to be saved. None of the nice people in first soil know Christ; they therefore are lost.

But an individual doesn't have to stay stuck in his or her own mud. You can change soils. There are three other options. Picking soil two, however, won't help at all.

Dirt #2

Let's dip back into the bag. I have an ancient Atari cartridge. It's from days of antiquity, from the seventies. Do you recall Combat? Remember, the little tanks shooting each other and spinning around when they got hit?

My dad gave us the video game when it first came out and my son and I played it incessantly. We hardly even took potty breaks. For two months I don't remember doing much of anything else. But then other games came along and so did other interests. It's now been fifteen years since I've played Combat, and yet, it's virtually all I did for two months. Would you call me a Combat player?

That's easy. I played Combat, but I'm not a player. I'm not committed to the game. I played it for only two months. Other things became more important to me.

But I *am* a basketball player. I played in junior high, high school, college, city leagues, AAU, and even professionally with the Los Angeles Lakers. I coached five years at the college level. I'm fifty years old, and during the previous five years I worked out with the Corvallis High School Spartans and helped coach their big men. I can still beat most people one-on-one. And I dunked on each of my birthdays except this one. One day, and I think it's coming soon, my back and other body parts that are wearing out won't allow me to play. But my heart is in the game. I'll follow it in the paper and I'll watch it on television. And when my eyes are gone, I'll listen to it on the radio. Anyone who knows me knows I am a basketball player. There is no doubt in anyone's mind, especially mine.

Although I've played Atari Combat, I'm not a Combat player. You can tell. I don't care much about it. I haven't played in fifteen years. People who play Christianity and quit are not Christians.[31] Christians keep playing.

The Bible tells us the condition of spiritual Atari players:

> The one who received the seed that fell on rocky places is the man who hears the word and at once receives it with joy. But since he has no root, he lasts only a short time. When trouble or persecution comes because of the word, he quickly falls away (Matthew 13:20-21).

A parallel passage confirms where second soil is headed:

> And in a similar way these are the ones on whom seed was sown on the rocky places, who, when they hear the word, immediately receive it with joy (Mark 4:16, NASB).

"And in a similar way" refers back to the first soil. In other words, the second soil's condition is the same as that of the first. Since Dirt #1 is going to hell, so is Dirt #2.

What about some people who go forward in church or at camp? They're given a prayer to read or repeat, get involved in Sunday school, are fired up for two months, and then drop out. Four years later they behave no differently from before they prayed the prayer. There hasn't been any behavior change since their two-month spiritual burp.

If you have a loved one who prayed the prayer but who isn't walking the walk, you at least have the hope that their prayer was sincere. But here are the cold hard facts: prayers are only words if our hearts don't match them. If you are double-minded when you pray, you don't have a prayer.

I don't know if I have illustrated second soil properly. I hope I haven't. The truth is, some people I really care about fit this scenario. They're nice. Some of them are terrific. But whatever Dirt #2 is, it is not going to heaven. It's a long shot if you're betting otherwise.

Flash-in-the-pan "Christians" are going to hell.

We are certain about Dirts #1 and #2. There is no doubt. We are also certain about Dirt #4. But we're not so sure about Dirt #3. For that reason we'll consider it after we see why soil four is considered clean dirt.

Dirt #4

I have a small Swiss Army knife in my bag of goodies. I use the blade to fix hangnails (watch out for the cuticle) and anything else that needs cutting. I use the file blade to smooth the rough edges of my freshly cut fingernails (I don't want jagged borders) and the pointed end to clean them (ugh, something green). It has a small pair of scissors that I use to keep my nose hairs trimmed. (When

I'm speaking there's nothing worse than having people in the front rows look up and think, *Ohhh, look at all those bushy nose hairs.*) My knife also has a pair of tweezers that I use for tweezing (works great on splinters), and a toothpick (ummm, sausage from breakfast). Frankly, I feel undressed when I forget to take my knife with me. I use it a lot. Would you call me a knife user?

Absolutely! There is no question about it. My knife is a part of my daily life.

Folks in fourth soil take the Lord into their daily lives and produce fruit:

> The one who received the seed that fell on good soil is the man who hears the word and understands it. He produces a crop, yielding a hundred, sixty or thirty times what was sown (Matthew 13:23).

Dirt four is made up of on-fire, goin'-for-it, no-holds-barred, Jesus-lovin' believers. And all of these folks are going to heaven. Their hearts are right with God and they want to walk with Him. Remember, it's the condition of the heart that distinguishes a person's standing with God, not what he does. When the heart changes, godly behavior will naturally begin to follow. It's guaranteed (*see* Romans 6).

Not doing good works is a pretty good sign you are not saved. Yet doing good works doesn't mean you are. Some people do good works in their own power. It happens all the time. Even though they are nice people who are working hard, if it isn't Christ producing the works through them, they won't qualify as soil four. There were unsaved people who called Jesus "Lord, Lord," who thought they were Christians, who were even doing miracles in His name (Matthew 7:21-23). God's Word will not come back void, no matter who preaches it, Christian or non-Christian. God was producing fruit in spite of them, but they had nothing to do with it.

> *Fourth soil folks let Jesus Christ do what He wants to through them, and they're the ones who are going to heaven for sure.*

So how do you know who's doing what?

We only know about ourselves. We can't be sure about anybody else. That's why we make such lousy fruit inspectors. We're so biased. I tend to think witnessing (oranges) is the best fruit and the only one that matters. But reading our Bible (cherries), praying (apples), caring for the poor (bananas), and ministering to prisoners (kiwi) are all kinds of fruit. So are counseling (pears), standing against political decisions that are contrary to Scripture (grapes), and cleaning the church (nectarines). All the other kinds of fruit I haven't mentioned count, too. But who is producing them, you or Jesus? You're Dirt #4 if it's Christ. And you can take that bet to the bank.

Judas looked like he was going to heaven. He walked with Jesus for three years. And Lot looked like he was going to hell, for sure. It's hard to be well-known in Las Vegas (Sodom) and not end up in the pit. But Judas went to hell, and Lot went to heaven. Sometimes it's hard to figure. Especially if you are Dirt #3 like Judas and Lot were. But don't worry—if you're Dirt #4, you're clean and you know it. But you won't know if you're Dirt #3.

Dirt #3

I have a small plastic ruler that I carry in my Bible along with an ink pen. I use it to underline significant passages of Scripture. You know how it is when you're in church and the preacher says, "Turn to the third chapter of John." It's important that the people next to you see the multicolored, coded underlining, and the margins full of notes and comments. They'll think, *Whew, he's spiritual!* And it's a good way to intimidate others. I just hate it when we're told to turn to Amos.

I've had the ruler four years, and I've faithfully used it three times a year. Usually I am in too much of a hurry to be neat. But I do use it occasionally.

Am I a ruler user?

That's a tough one. I'm not sure. And the Bible isn't much help either:

> The one who received the seed that fell among the thorns is the man who hears the word, but the worries of this life and the deceitfulness of wealth choke it, making it unfruitful (Matthew 13:22).

Fruit is not a proof of salvation, it is an indicator. Did this guy produce some friut earlier, or was there never any at all? Who knows?

It's hard to be in the world and not be a part of it. Yet that is the challenge for Christians. Personal ambition, goals, desires, dreams, and the quest for money, position, and power tend to replace Christ at the top of our value system. The cares of the world choke out our faith. Or do they? Did we ever have it in the first place? Who knows?

Can you be a Christian and have Jesus Christ be second place or lower? Sure. But your odds aren't good.

Is "once saved always saved" for real, or can you lose your salvation? It doesn't matter for those who love Jesus. It's a big question for those who don't.

All of these third soil issues are discussed in depth in my book *Something's Fishy*, so I'll just summarize my position here. Some of third soil goes to heaven, but most of it goes to hell. Those in it don't know where they are going until it's too late to do anything about it. Why? Because they're living in the fuzzy gray area of life.

How much do you have to use a ruler to be known as a ruler user? Who knows? There is an unknown element in the answer. We're in a gray area. And that's the problem with being a third soil person. You're living in the gray area and therefore can never know for sure where you are going.

It's easy to think you're a Christian and not be. That's the situation in which most third soil people find themselves—and most Christians identify with third soil.

Ananias, Sapphira, Simon the sorcerer, and Judas all hoped they would go to heaven. So did Lot. But none of them knew for sure until it was too late, and Scripture only confirms that one of them actually went—Lot.

How can a third soil person be sure? That's the catch—they can't.

As I have said, if you are betting on Soils #1 and #2 you are betting against the Bible being wrong. That dramatically reduces your odds on being right. If you are betting that Soil #3 is going to heaven, your odds are better than if you are betting on #1 or #2 because the Bible isn't clear regarding #3. Just don't forget to measure upside potential against downside risk. We're not risking dollars or pride on this bet. The winners go to heaven. The losers go to hell. That makes #3 a long shot.

I'm an old athlete, not very smart, and I'm hardly a theologian (I haven't even been to Bible school), but it seems to me that for those of us in the rank and file of Christendom, if the smart guys aren't sure about third soil, how can we be? Don't risk eternity on the conflicting opinions of the scholars. If you identify with any soil other than #4, you are taking a monumental chance. Why take it? Eternity is on the line.

Take a Fresh Look at the Cross

Did you identify with third soil? If you did, do you want to get out? I have news for you. You can't work hard enough to escape. What's the answer? Take a fresh look at the cross. Salvation is an issue of the heart. God would like to change yours. Do you want Him to? Take a good look at Jesus.

Move over to fourth ground. The consequences of being the wrong kind of dirt are too severe. Remember, all dirt goes into eternal storage when the life goes out of it. Clean dirt goes one direction and dirty dirt goes the other.

There are all kinds of people represented in first soil. Good and bad, terrific and terrible, but they know who they are. They have rejected Jesus Christ. If the whole deal is real, they are all doomed to hell—and being nice has nothing to do with where they are going.

The same is true of second soil. I know some wonderful people who seem to be in that category, some of whom I love deeply. They, too, will go to hell if the whole deal is real. All of them!

Most of third soil is made up of nice people. Not all of them will end up in hell if the whole deal is real, but a great number will.

I know some good people who are Dirt #4. And I know some I don't like much. As I mentioned before, Christianity would be great if it weren't for Christians. I've got some first soil friends I'd rather spend time with than some stuffy fourth soil believers who have been weaned on pickle juice. But personality doesn't have any more to do with it than works do. The issue is the heart.

If you have a passion for God and His Son Jesus Christ, you are fourth soil and are heaven-bound.

If you don't, you are some other soil and may be in big trouble.

Changing Soils

What if you aren't fourth soil? Lots of nice people aren't. Can you change or does God change you?

Yes!

Isn't that a fun answer? But it's not an easy one. I believe both you and God play a role. Not everyone agrees with me. Theologians argue about the sovereignty of God and the free will of man.

Can God do whatever He wants whenever He wants?

Sure! Although He can't sin, He is still God. He's sovereign.

So can He help an unsaved person receive Christ as Savior?

Yes.

Does He?

To some degree. No person comes to salvation without the pulling of the Father (*see* John 6:44). God chooses us.

But does He violate a person's choice?

That's where the argument comes in. We know that He doesn't want any to perish and that He wants all to repent (*see* 2 Peter 3:9). But we also know that most are perishing—most are choosing to reject Jesus Christ (*see* Matthew 7:13-14).

So we have to conclude that although God is sovereign, He doesn't run roughshod over people or there wouldn't be so many perishing. Therefore, we must have some choice in the matter. God influences those He chooses, and we respond. But when we don't respond, He allows us to remain in our sins.

So how does God influence us?

Lots of ways. He'll use people, the Bible and other books, nature, church, preaching, and prayer. And He'll use the hard circumstances of life as a means of discipline. But then if you don't receive Christ, you'll get punishment.

Do fourth soil believers who start to slip in their faith get punished?

No, they get disciplined.

What about third soil folks?

Both third soil believers and nonbelievers get discipline for awhile. Those who don't believe ultimately get punishment.

What's the difference?

Discipline or Punishment?

Our daughter Kim was an expert at figuring reasons to get out of bed while in her terrible twos. Every night, first it was, "I forgot to kiss you goodnight," then, "I forgot to get a drink," followed by, "We didn't pray for Grandma" (or whoever we hadn't prayed for), and on and on and on. Finally, one night I'd had it and I issued an ultimatum.

"If you get out of bed for any reason, any reason at all," I said firmly, "I will spank you."

As soon as I walked out of the bedroom and settled in my chair in the living room I heard her door open and saw a little face peek around the door jamb, her eyes looking down the hall. For effect she gave a couple of blinks flashing those big baby blues and quietly asked, "But what if I have to throw up?"

There was no holding back the laughter, no matter how hard we tried. Our lips pursed together at first as our bodies wiggled and convulsed at the laughing going on inside, but finally it had to come out. Spray and sputter gushed forth as Mary and I finally let it go. It was the sound little Kimmy had been waiting for. She came running and flew onto my lap knowing she was safe. I never could spank her when I was laughing. You can also see the challenge set before me as a father.

As a Christian you need to understand that there will never be punishment for you. Christ took all the castigation for your sin. There will be discipline, but there's no punishment. Here's the difference:

Your young son throws a fit in an aisle of a crowded supermarket and mops the floor with his body as he writhes and screams, demanding a candy bar. Let's assume you counter his behavior with the sound of one hand clapping . . . on the seat of his understanding. Why did you spank him? If the swats to his posterior were the consequence or penalty for acting like that in a public place, or because you were embarrassed, you punished him. If, however, before you left home for the store, you had told him there would be no candy bar today and warned him about his temper—as an attempt to break his tendency to throw fits—and if your desire was to alter his behavior so that he would act properly in public places, the shots to his bottom were discipline.

Discipline is concerned with modifying future behavior. Punishment is a penalty and has no concern for the future. Discipline is used to alter behavior for both believers and unbelievers. Punishment is not a process. It is situationally unchanging.

Punishment is reserved for the unbeliever who, after repeated discipline, has rejected God's Son. It will come in the severest form possible—hell! That's the ultimate form of retribution.

If you do not have salvation, God will continue to work the circumstances of life to draw you to Christ.[32] That's discipline. He wants to change your heart. Usually He uses hard encounters. That tends to get the best results.

God will do the same for the believer. He continues the process of molding us into the image of His Son using life's problems. Just remember, this process of influencing through hard circumstances is discipline, not punishment. If you know Jesus Christ as your Savior, God will never punish you. Christ has taken upon Himself your punishment—past, present, and future.

But for believers and nonbelievers alike, the discipline you receive from your heavenly Father will be determined by how deeply rebellion is entrenched in your life.

How Deep Are Your Rebellious Roots?

When a teenager decides to rebel against God by dishonoring his parents, discipline will often come in some form or another, usually including some kind of restriction. If he doesn't respond, he may try drugs or stealing as his next expression of rebellion. Time in a correctional school might be next for him. If he doesn't respond, his next foul-up may be followed by prison, from low to maximum security and heavy labor to solitary confinement, depending on the depth of his rebellious nature.

Discipline comes in degrees according to the depth of rebellion, and is designed to break the will. But sometimes a person refuses to be broken, even though it is God who is administering the discipline.

> *The more deeply a sin is rooted in a life, the greater will be the degree of discipline used to alter the behavior patterns.*

It's not wise to fight God when it comes to your rebellious roots. Remember His words, "My son, do not reject the discipline of the LORD, or loathe His reproof, for whom the LORD loves He reproves, even as a father, the son in whom He delights" (Proverbs 3:11-12, NASB).

Whether we're Christian or non-Christian, God is primarily concerned with our rebellious hearts. But believers have three additional factors for discipline to contend with: 1) how long you've known the Lord; 2) the depth of your calling; and 3) the kind of sin committed.

Short-Timer or Long-Timer?

When Moses first started out in the ministry, God said, "Go to Pharaoh and tell him to let My people go."

Do you know what Moses did? Five times he tried to get out of going.

First he said, "Oh God, I'm not worthy of going before Pharaoh." It was his first word of rebellion.

"Don't worry about it, Moses. I'll make sure everything's okay, just go."

"But I won't know what to say," Moses whined. Disobedience again.

"Just go, I'll give you the words."

"But what if he won't listen to me?" Moses replied in his third revolt.

"I'll make sure he listens, Moses. Just go."

"Well God, you know I stammer a bit; I'm not eloquent, and I do have a little problem with my speech," complained Moses, demonstrating his lack of faith for the fourth time.

God was getting perturbed. "Moses, will you just trust Me and go?"

By now Moses had run out of excuses: "God, would you just send somebody else?"

"No," God spoke firmly, "I'll send somebody with you—but you gotta' go."

What were the consequences of Moses' rebellion?

Having two bosses in the camp (Moses and his brother Aaron) brought about the whole golden calf scenario, which probably wouldn't have happened without an Aaron present. But were there any overt, personal consequences to Moses that you can think of? No, at least none that are recorded. How come? I think it was because he was brand new at what he was doing. He was new in the ministry. Although he'd had forty years of seasoning he was still green as grass.

Ladies, are you better cooks today than you were when you first started? I hope so! Gentlemen, are you better husbands today than when you first got married? You ought to be; you've had time to practice. What about Moses? He was brand new at what he was doing and God knew it.

I'm not preaching cheap grace, so please don't misunderstand me. But, if you're brand new in the faith,

God's pretty patient. He's gentle and understanding, and there's a little room to mess up without the consequences being too severe. That's good news if you are just getting started in your Christian walk. You're responsible for a pregnancy out of wedlock, contracting a sexually transmitted disease, or a traumatic car accident from drinking and driving. Don't blame those on God. But typically, early foul-ups rarely have long-lasting consequences. You've got God's Word on it: "The LORD is slow to anger, abounding in love and forgiving sin and rebellion" (Numbers 14:18a).

How long you've known the Lord is just one factor determining God's response to your sin. The depth of His calling is another.

Big Shots Fall the Hardest

Do you remember later on when Moses was mature in his faith? It was the second rock-calling contest.

God said, "Moses, the folks are thirsty and are starting to grumble again. Hold your staff up in the air and call water out of that rock."

I happen to know it was a Monday. You know, one of those blue, awful Mondays. Moses was really tired of these turkeys. They had just finished another lap around Mt. Sinai. And he was tired of doing tricks. Quite frankly, he was fed up with his staff.

Sure, his rod could gobble up other staffs that looked like snakes, it could make water part, it could bring in a covey of quail, and he could win battles just by holding it up in the air. But now, on blue Monday, God wanted him to do another trick with it. But Moses was tired of doing tricks.

Moses thought, *I wonder when God will want me to sit up and go fetch? I'm fed up with laps, I'm tired of dealing with these rebellious turkeys, I'm sick of doing tricks, and I don't want to hold this stinking stick up in the air and yell at some dumb rock.*

It was just one of those little moments a person sometimes has on a Monday. We've all had them.

He continued thinking, *All right, I gotta' do it 'cause God's gonna' make me do it, but I ain't calling no water outta' no rock. I'm gonna' smack it out.*

So Moses took his rod and gave the rock a couple of whacks as he yelled, "Come on out, water!" And when the water came out Moses smirked and siphoned off some of God's glory when he said, "Look what we did."

Moses was a mature man of faith by now. He was Numero Uno in the land, but he had dishonored God in front of the people over whom he had charge. And to boot, he had siphoned off some of the glory. Do you remember the consequences of Moses' behavior?

God told Moses, "Go up on that mountain over there and look at the promised land . . . because you're never going to set foot in it. And after you've finished looking it will be time for you to die" (*see* Numbers 20:7-12; Deuteronomy 1-5).

I think Moses took a very long look.

My calling is a high one. I'm a speaker, author, and church consultant. I talk to over twenty-thousand people a year, so you won't catch me questioning God on this one, but that always seemed harsh to me. I couldn't understand why God was so tough on Moses—after all, it was a Monday. But then I began to understand the importance of Moses' position and the domino effect that could occur in the ranks if God had let him get away with it. That was when I understood: watch out, the dominoes fall when leadership falls.

If you are a Sunday school teacher, a Bible study leader, an elder, a pastor, or if you hold any ministry position with charge or authority over people, you are a person with a high calling. You have responsibility for the growth and well-being of a flock, just like Moses. You have a high-priestly function in that you represent God to them, and them to God. I am not suggesting any violation of the individual priesthood of the believer. I'm just making you aware of the responsibilities that come with discipleship (growing in Christ) and I'm warning you. Don't mess up! The consequences are too severe, especially if your position involves responsibility for others.

Position usually fosters pride. That's the downside of responsibility. Remember, "God opposes the proud but gives grace to the humble" (James 4:6; *see* 1 Peter 5:5).

What You Do Does Matter

God is God and we're not. We make ourselves out to be God when we do our thing and not His. That's why all sin has its roots in rebellion. There is only one sin: saying no to God. There are many ways of expressing it. That's why if you haven't passed your sin on to Christ, the long-term results will condemn you to what the Bible calls hell. If you don't have a personal relationship with Christ, God has no choice but to exclude you from His presence.

Sin also has short-term consequences. Although there is no hierarchy up and down the spectrum of sin, there are two at the top that seem to matter to God more than the rest. Those who choose to violate the biggies tend to get a heavier hand from God.

If you are a leader who is mature in your faith, don't fall to immorality. Very few ever fully recover. The apostle Paul made it clear. Sexual sin is in a league by itself:

> Flee from sexual immorality. All other sins a man commits are outside his body, but he who sins sexually sins against his own body. Do you not know that your body is a temple of the Holy Spirit, who is in you, whom you have received from God? You are not your own; you were bought at a price. Therefore honor God with your body (1 Corinthians 6:18-20).

God hates sexual sin and deals out discipline for it with the toughest of measures.[33]

Idol worship is the other biggie. God called it spiritual adultery. All the rest seem to get about the same amount of God's attention. So don't value money, things, goals, or desires more than the things of God. They all represent false idols and will bring you down.

Are you being disciplined by God? If you are already dirt four, He will keep working to improve your soil. If not, He wants you to change soils.

The goal of discipline is to change your heart.

Is He trying to change you? Let Him. As a Christian you'll miss the fun of bearing the fruit of the Spirit if you resist change, and receive God's discipline in the process. If you're not a Christian, you'll get punishment. And you know what that means by now—no matter how nice you are.

Chapter Six

WHO GOES WHERE AND WHY? (If the whole deal is real, nice people really do go to hell.)

"I can be a good person and get myself into heaven," is the philosophy of most. "Nice people don't really go to hell," is the prevailing thought. And it seems right. But then, there are lots of things that seem right to us that aren't right with God (*see* Proverbs 14:12).

God's ways may seem a little strange. Having to trust someone else with our eternal destiny seems bizarre. That's what we have to do when we rely on Christ to resolve our sin. (Remember, it's our sin problem that causes us a hell problem.) Why can't we resolve the issue of heaven or hell on our own?

How good would a person have to be to get into heaven without help? Perfect! Because that's what God is, and heaven is where He is.

Are you perfect? No, you're an onion. You stink. Sin does that to a person.

We're All Onions

The next time you're with friends sniff 'em. Really! Just give them a big sniff. Check out their scents.

Let me tell you what you'll smell. You will either smell their stink, or you will smell something covering up their stink. Why? Because we all stink. It is our nature. Sin creates stench. We all have sin, therefore we all reek. You got your dad's stink, and you gave yours to your kids. Face it. You're an onion.

What happens when you put an onion in the refrigerator? It stinks up everything inside. That's why you can't go to heaven as an onion. If you could you would stink up high heaven.

Imagine yourself on the family room floor and someone opens the refrigerator door. What comes wafting across the room with the cold air from the 'fridge? Stink! The onions have done it again. But how badly they stink depends on the kind of onion.

Bermuda onions are just about the worst. Eat a big slice on a burger just before bedtime. Talk about morning mouth! Your dog will especially love you.

Walla Walla onions don't stink like other onions. They're the best. So are Maui onions. People argue over which variety has the least odor.

Leeks, chives, and red and green onions are somewhere in between.

We measure stink by comparing onions to onions. But that's the wrong standard. We think Walla Wallas and Mauis are the best because they stink the least. But any onion will still ruin the food in a refrigerator, including the two least stinky. The standard is not which onions stink the least.

God's standard is the absence of stink of any kind.

God is holy and pure. It doesn't stink where He is. So nobody who does stink, even just a little bit, is going there.

Man was created in God's image, but that doesn't make God an onion. We didn't become onions until Adam and Eve uttered the first no to Him. Sin and death were the result, and that was the origin of our sin nature. Adam was made in the image of God. We were born in the image of Adam, with a sin nature. From that point on we were disqualified from heaven on the basis of our own merit. Why? Because as onions we would make heaven stink.

Let me summarize:

1) We stink.

2) Stink isn't possible in heaven.

That creates a serious problem. What can be done? I'm an onion and I wanna go to heaven. The first option is cooking. Cooking an onion will get rid of some of its stink.

The first chance you get, sniff an old person. Just walk up and sniff 'em. You'll notice that he doesn't smell as bad as a younger individual. Why? Because life has cooked some of the stink out of 'em. But cooking doesn't completely solve an onion's odor problem, because a cooked onion will still stink up a refrigerator.

Since cooking won't eliminate completely an onion's stink, ultimately God is faced with one of two decisions: 1) Dispose of it. Throw it in the trash or grind it up in the disposal—hell. That's what I am trying to warn you about. Don't let it happen to you, or to the nice people you know.

Or, 2) wrap it in Saran Wrap, cling wrap, Handi Wrap, or zip-lock that sucker. That will do it. Then you can put it in the refrigerator as long as you need to and it won't stink up the place.

I never could understand the idea of my sin being covered by the blood of Christ. It seemed so gross. Drip, drip, drip. Then the Handi Wrap of Christ concept came to mind. It was close to being correct, but it just missed the mark. Having an onion under the wrapping, I had described how animal sacrifices worked during Old Testament times—as a temporary covering until Christ could complete the work on the cross. But I had missed the New Testament concept.

When we place our faith in Christ we are new creatures in Him—new creations, spiritual birth has taken place, we are born again. So to make the wrapping concept correct, we have to imagine an onion wrapped in Saran Wrap. Then unwrap it. When the onion layers are peeled off, what would you expect to find? Nothing, because an onion is nothing more than stinky layers. But something happens when you wrap up in the Handi Wrap of Christ. A miracle occurs. The onion is given a core. A perfect piece of fruit is created in its center. And it grows as you conform to the image of His Son, eliminating onion layers from the inside out. After a while there are only a few stinky layers wrapped around the outside of the fruit. Some scholars call the layers that remain flesh—old worldly habit patterns left over from living in this world. Others call the layers the remains of our sin nature.

Regardless of what it's called, the source of the stink that remains is what the apostle Paul struggled with in Romans 7:15-25. A paraphrase goes something like this; "I wish I hadn't done what I just did. Why did I do it? I didn't want to. But I did it anyway. I don't want to do it again, but I probably will. Why do I do the things I don't want to do? There is something in me that fights with what I ought to do." Paul is describing the remaining layers of onion wrapped around the fruit that had been created when spiritual birth occurred.

Even though there is a little onion left on those of us who know Christ, just remember, God has X-ray vision. When He looks He sees the apple or orange or pear or whatever piece of fruit He created—the new creature in Christ. It's the fruit that goes to heaven to await its joining with a new body. And that new spiritual body has had the last of its onion layers peeled off.

Onions don't go to heaven. But you were born an onion. And you can't get into heaven unless you're some kind of fruit, or unless you are perfect (with no smell). Since you already smell, the second option is not possible. You really have only one choice. Wrap up in Christ and let Him create fruit, or go to hell

Perhaps an understanding of perfection will further illustrate this point.

Are You Perfect?

Watterson's *Calvin and Hobbes* is one of my favorite comic strips. Just prior to Christmas[34] Calvin is on the front of his sled, his come-to-life stuffed tiger Hobbes is on the back, and they are having a discussion.

Calvin begins, "I'm getting nervous about Christmas."

Hobbes answers with a question, "You're worried you haven't been good?"

"That's just the question. It's all relative. What's Santa's definition? How good do you have to be to qualify as good?"

Calvin has just asked a big-time question. He continues as they zoom between trees on their way down the hill: "I haven't killed anybody. See, that's good, right? I haven't committed any felonies. I didn't start any wars. I don't practice cannibalism. Wouldn't you say that's pretty good? Wouldn't you say I should get lots of presents?"

Hobbes offers a deep thought and probes with his reply, "But maybe good is more than the absence of bad."

It's a thought Calvin has considered. "See, that's what worries me."

Calvin doesn't know how good "good" really is. But he wants to tip the scales in his favor. So he asks Hobbes, "Okay, assuming I can get an overnight letter to the North Pole, what would you charge to write me a glowing character reference?"

Hobbes knows Calvin's heart. You can tell by his response, "Oh no, I'm not going to perjure myself for you! My record's clean."

Neither one of them is sure what good is, but both are pretty sure Calvin is not whatever it is. However, Hobbes thinks his record is clean and is therefore okay. He considers himself to be good. Both have concluded that being good is a relative term.

Everything is relative to a standard. Time is measured by a single clock kept in Greenwich, England, and all other clocks around the world are set in accordance with the one that is considered to be the standard. Your timepiece is accurate only when it is set exactly with the one that serves as the gauge for measurement. The Bureau of Weights and Measures keeps the standards by which all the other weights and volumes around our country are measured. Your scale is accurate only when it weighs exactly the same as the standard kept at the bureau.

We cannot afford the technology necessary to keep our measurement devices in tune with the standards at the bureau. Temperature, moisture, pressure, corrosion, and all the other factors altering a perfect environment are too difficult and expensive for us to maintain. So we settle for something that is within acceptable limits. In other words, something less than the standard. Concepts like *good*, *better*, *best*, *nice*, and *good enough* are the result. Comparisons are being made to a standard when such words are used. But none of these ideas have any meaning apart from the standard that defines them.

Something other than the standard is perfect only when it is in every way equivalent to the standard. God is perfect. So is Jesus Christ. Both serve as representations of the same standard of perfection.

God's standard is Christ. All comparisons are made to Him. But we tend to think that nice is good enough because we make our comparisons to each other.

With time, weights, and measures we determine what is close enough for the need. Thus the word *tolerances*. Building a house requires less precision than building a shuttle craft. You need a more accurate thermometer to measure the heat generated in a high performance racing engine than in an oven baking a turkey. We settle for less than perfection because perfection is either not possible or too expensive to achieve. But God doesn't acknowledge tolerances in heaven. *Close enough* is a human term. Let me explain what I'm trying to say, using baseball as an analogy.

Is There a Baseball Heaven?

Columnist George Will called it "The Season of '41." Ted Williams and Joe DiMaggio went on a tear. Williams hit today's equivalent of .419. DiMaggio hit safely in fifty-six consecutive games. In his article in

Newsweek Will said this of Ted Williams:

> Williams used a postal scale in the clubhouse to make sure humidity had not increased the weight of his bats. An official of the Louisville Slugger company once challenged Williams to pick the one bat among six that weighed half an ounce more than the other five. He did. He once sent back to the factory a shipment of bats because he sensed the handles were too thick. They were, by .005 of an inch.
>
> Williams was hitting .39955 going into the season-ending doubleheader in Philadelphia's Shibe Park. Daylight savings had ended the night before, so the autumn shadows that made hitting hard there would be even worse. If Williams had not played, his average would have been rounded to .400. Instead, he went 6 for 8, including a blazing double that broke a public address speaker. He finished at .406. Today when a batter hits a sacrifice fly he is not charged with an at bat. In 1941 he was. William's manager, Joe Cronin, estimates Williams hit 14 of them, so under today's rules his average would have been .419. Since then, the highest average was George Brett's .390 in 1980.[15]

Williams' achievement is one of the greatest in baseball history. Imagine! He got on base over 40 percent of the time. If there is a baseball heaven, considering all the people who have ever played, he must be there.

In baseball, perfection is getting on base with each trip to the plate. It's called batting a thousand. But nobody has ever done that beyond a game or two, and certainly not for an entire season. So we need terms like *good, better, best, nice,* and *good enough* to determine who gets to the big leagues, who makes the most money, and who gets into the Hall of Fame. These are the tolerances of baseball.

Over the course of history, hitters batting .400 have been rare indeed. There have been a few and they are considered the best of baseball. Ted Williams was the last to do it. By the way, they didn't have to do much else well. If you can hit .400 or better you don't have to be a good fielder and you will still be considered the best.

You can also be numbered among the best and hit .300 or better, if a lot of your hits are home runs. Even low .300 hitters are called the best if they can hit under pressure and drive in lots of runs. But they usually have to be pretty good in the field too. And the best almost always get elected into the baseball Hall of Fame.

Better sluggers hit in the high .200s. Good hitters do a little better than .250. Nice players hit close to .250, but they have to be excellent fielders and role players.

Being good enough is the big qualifier. You are good enough when you get out of the minors. Making the majors is the most important step of all, whether or not you play. Staying out of the minor leagues is very important to a professional baseball player. Being a big leaguer is crucial and every player strives to be good enough to make it to the "bigs."

Using baseball criteria, who goes to heaven and who goes to hell? Is the break at best, better, good, or nice? What is good enough? Maybe hell is the minors and heaven is the majors. Or are only Hall of Famers in heaven and the rest in hell? The problem is, all of these divisions are based on comparisons between ballplayers, not the standard—which is hitting a thousand.

"But," you say, "the moment you compare them to the standard nobody qualifies." And that's the point! It's what I've been saying all along. Rex Harrison would say, "By Jove, I think you've got it." There are some real nice people who won't qualify, right?

You should realize by now that there are some pretty good baseball players who never even make it to the minors. There are some nice players who never make it from the minors to the majors. And there are some exceptionally good players in the big leagues who never make it into the Hall of Fame. But they all have one thing in common, including those who are in the hall. None of them ever batted a thousand, and in that regard they're just like those of us who never played baseball.

In reality, going to heaven or hell is nothing like playing in the major leagues as opposed to the minors. Why not? Because none got on base every time they were at bat. Heaven can't be equated to making the baseball Hall of Fame either, because the hall is filled with players who, although they were the best at what they did, weren't perfect when they did it.

There are only two ways to get into heaven using baseball as our analogy. The first, bat a thousand over your whole career. That will get you in for sure. The problem is, only one guy ever did it.

Jesus Christ was never put out . . . not in Pee Wee baseball, not in Little League, not in American Legion, not in the minors, and not during His three years in the big leagues. He was the best. He hit a thousand and never made an error. Nobody ever accomplished what He did, and none have done it since. The Bible says no one will ever do it again. All but Jesus Christ have struck out and come short of the perfection of God (*see* Romans 3:23).

Good, better, best, nice, and good enough are terms we use to compare ourselves with each other. But God is the standard and Jesus is our model of perfection. And no person will ever measure up to Jesus because of Adam's sin in us all. So batting a thousand becomes an impossible way to enter the kingdom of God.

So the first way into heaven really isn't a way in at all. It's impossible to be good or nice enough. Using the comparison rationale, we have to conclude nice people do go to hell.

The second way to get into heaven is to be on the right team. During my coaching days, *the* team in the world of college basketball was UCLA. John Wooden won ten NCAA championships in twelve years and became a legend. Being on his staff was the ultimate coaching experience.

Being on the Lakers' team was the ultimate playing experience. In the last twenty-four years there have been only seven years when either the Los Angeles Lakers or the Boston Celtics haven't been in the championship series, and one or the other has won the crown in all but nine of those years. Los Angeles and Boston have been in a league all their own. It was fun being a part of it. I made it to the NBA and was on one of the two best teams in the history of the game. If we had scored three more points in that seventh playoff game I'd have a big ol' world championship ring on my nose pickin' finger. I'd flash it as much as I could.

In baseball making the majors is a big deal. But using our analogy, it's not a big deal to God. Getting into the big leagues is not the equivalent of heaven, because being on any ol' team won't solve your problem. Unless you're perfect, you have to be on Jesus' team, or you don't qualify for the kingdom. It's just like onions. Either don't stink or wrap up. With the Lakers I was on a great team. But only Boston won the championship that year. I didn't qualify for a ring because I was on the wrong team.

Through onions, measurements, baseball, and basketball, I have tried to show you how we tend to make comparisons to each other, rather than to the standard of God, when determining what's good enough. Yet perhaps you are struggling with the issue of whether God is fair. If that's a problem, perhaps three definitions, along with a few illustrations, will help clear things up.

Justice (Getting What We Deserve)

Years ago at a Christian Camping International meeting I heard Stuart Briscoe define justice as getting what we deserve, mercy as not getting all we deserve, and grace as getting something we don't deserve at all. Let's start with justice and try to understand why we don't want it.

As I was proofreading this portion of the manuscript, I happened to be flying from New York to Denver. The in-flight movie was *Defending Your Life*. The plot caught my attention. It was timely, so I added the following review.

The star is killed in a car wreck and wakes up in Judgment City. A defender and a prosecutor are assigned to his case, along with two judges to rule on whether he has to go back to earth in another life, or press on as a citizen of the universe to begin learning to use more and more of his brain. You can't become a citizen until you're able to conquer your fears. Selected portions of his past were reviewed on videotape and then debated.

While in Judgment City, he meets a woman who is a good person and who has her fears under control. They fall in love, and during their last night together she invites him to sleep with her. He decides not to for several reasons, including being fearful of what it might do to them wherever they end up going next.

According to the movie, the "right thing" was to make love to this woman, but instead, he is condemned for doing the right thing, which was refusing. So the result of their evaluation was: she would be moved on, but he wouldn't pass because he still had fear.

It's not surprising that neither heaven nor hell exists in the universe that is portrayed. Denial prevails. Nor should I expect morality to be considered a virtue (this is, after all, a Hollywood production). The only criteria for moving on is being a "good" person and overcoming your fears. God has nothing to do with anything.

In the movie, if you hadn't sufficiently conquered your fears, you got justice (which was going back to earth as many times as it took for you to get it right). That New Age treatment is a long way from a biblical scenario.

People who don't understand the God of the Bible somehow convince themselves that His love will overcome the mandate of His holiness—which demands that He carry out justice. Judgment City in the Bible is the Great White Throne, where there is no trial or debate. There will be no going back until you get it right.

Justice demands an irreversible hell.

As a result of that understanding, I don't want you to overcome your fear. In fact, my preference is that you be overcome by it. Be afraid for yourself if you don't know Christ! Be terrified for your friends who don't know him. It will be a natural outcome if you understand the truth.

Assume I am the star player on a high-school basketball team and I'm out with a really cute girl. Curfew is at 10:00 P.M. It is now 9:40 P.M. I have a decision to make.

The penalty for breaking curfew is a chewing out by the coach and running twenty laps. I want to kiss this girl goodnight, but I need more time. She's not ready to lay a lippy on me yet.

The chewing out is no big deal, and having run twenty laps at other times in my basketball career, I know what that feels like. I can handle it. But I have never kissed this girl before; I don't know what that feels like. And if I take her home now, I don't think she'll kiss me. I need a little more time.

I ponder for a few moments, *What to do, what to do? Twenty laps is tough . . . but the girl is really cute*. Naturally I decide to go for it and to take whatever I have coming to me at tomorrow's workout.

The next day at basketball practice, the coach says, "Carty, judging by the smile on your face, you broke curfew last night. Is that true?"

"Yes sir," I reply with a grin of satisfaction.

"Well, don't stand there talking. Start running, we'll talk later."

Consider these questions:

Who made the rules?

Sure, the coach.

Who chose to break the rules?

I did.

Did the coach decide I would run twenty laps, or did I?

I made the decision; the coach just enforced the rule.

Some people say, "How can a loving God send so many people to hell?"

Consider these questions as a response:

Who made the rules of life?

God did.

Who breaks His rules?

We do.

Who decides who goes to hell?

We do! God just enforces the rules. In other words, we do the sending.

Lewis Sperry Chafer said, "The marvel of it all is not that sinners are lost, but that they are ever saved."[36] In other words, we shouldn't be surprised that nice people really do go to hell.

Justice is getting what we deserve. And nice people deserve justice as much as anybody else. Baseball and onions prove that.

Understand one thing clearly. God does not want you to go to hell. His desire is to spend eternity with you. "The Lord is not slow in keeping his promise, as some understand slowness. He is patient with you, not wanting anyone to perish, but everyone to come to repentance" (2 Peter 3:9).

It's hard to believe that God wants to spend eternity with any of us, isn't it? I know what I can be in my private times. I know what I am deep down inside, and I don't like it much. Some of the stuff that comes out of my nature is disgusting. And you know what you are. Some of your thoughts are terrible, too. What's scary is that we are capable of such awfulness. We're onions. Yet, God wants to spend eternity with us. God loves us, but He will let us have our own way. If it's separation we want, it's separation we'll get. Left to our own devices, we'll get what we deserve . . . justice. And justice means hell.

Do yourself a favor. Don't ever get pious and pray for justice.

The last thing in the world you want from God is what you have coming to you.

Think about it. What if God were to give you what you deserve? I don't want Him to be just with me. I want my past forgotten. Judge me on the basis of some other criterion, because judgment based on my past means hellfire for sure. No sir, when it comes to sin I don't want to get what I deserve. I'm an onion and I stink!

There you are, probably sitting comfortably as you read. Although you deserve justice, nothing has happened to you . . . yet. Time continues to pass, and nothing is happening. So if you don't know Christ, unless you die in the next few moments, what you are experiencing is mercy.

Mercy is a little extra time for you to lay hold of grace, so you don't have to endure justice. Keep reading while I explain.

Mercy (Not Getting All You Deserve)

There I am, the basketball player who broke curfew, running my laps. As I finish my tenth trip around the floor, the coach looks over and yells, "Carty, how many laps have you run?"

Panting, I holler, "Ten."

Then he says, "Sit down Jay; rest awhile and I'll see if I can find someone else to run the other ten for you."

I was supposed to run twenty laps, but the coach let me rest after ten. What a guy! That's mercy . . . not getting all I deserved.

Do understand, this illustration does not apply to hell. It's impossible to run ten laps in hell and get out for the other ten. The Bible makes it clear: once you're there, you're there.

But the story does apply in this way. I'll bet you are well fed. Probably better than you ought to be. And you are most likely living in a decent apartment or house. Nicer than most people in the world. And you are well clothed, at least by the world's standards. In other words, things aren't too bad for you right now. Sure, your situation could be better. There are a few hassles in your life. But compared to most people, things could also be much worse. Isn't that right?

If, as you are reading this, you do not have a personal relationship with Jesus Christ, I have good news for you.

Unless you die in the next few moments, God has given you a little more time—more time to find Christ.

In other words, you're not getting all you deserve. You deserve justice, but He's giving you more time to respond to Christ. That's called mercy. But grace is something totally different.

Grace (Getting Something We Don't Deserve)

Our basketball player shows up the next day after breaking curfew and the coach asks him about staying out late. The player tells all.

Here's the problem. The rule is fixed. To not enforce the rule makes the coach a liar, which he is not. Everybody knows that. Twenty laps have to be run. That is the penalty.

To the surprise of the player, and the whole team as well, the coach says, "Sit down son, I'll run your laps for you."

I've played basketball for lots of coaches over the years. And I can tell you for sure, not once has a coach ever even thought about running my laps for me, let alone done it. Yet that is exactly what Jesus Christ did for us. While we were still onions, Christ ran our laps (*see* Romans 5:8).

God gives you two choices: 1) pay the price for your sins (justice); or 2) accept the payment that was made on your behalf (grace). Do you remember the song, "He paid a debt He did not owe; I owed a debt I could not pay"? Jesus paid our debt so we wouldn't have to. What was our part in the deal? Nothing; we're onions.

We were both the reason for and the beneficiaries of the death of our Lord. God chose to save us, even though we caused the debt He paid. Wow! We don't deserve it, but He did it anyhow. And in spite of what we are, Jesus Christ is looking forward to spending eternity with each person who chooses to follow Him. He wants to serve you.

We will worship Him, but He will serve us. He washed the disciples' feet as an example of servant leadership. The same will be true in heaven. Christ will actually serve us there. I cried when I realized that. Wow! That's a great, big, double WOW! That's grace.

Keep this in mind. Grace is offered to all people, the good as well as the bad. It's available to folks who seem to be better than some and to those who aren't perceived as being good enough by others. Christ died for nice people and for those who aren't so nice. And He did it because God can't love in degrees. He can only love perfectly. That means He loves us all the same, regardless of what we've done. So He died for all people in all walks of life who will accept what He did, regardless of the comparisons we make with each other.

What about nice people who don't accept Christ's payment on their behalf? You guess'ter Chester—unless they're perfect, they go to hell. Being nice has nothing to do with anything eternal. And the odds on that not being true are the same as the odds on the central theme of the Bible being wrong.

The Righteousness Scale

Pause for a moment and think of two names. Excluding Bible characters, who is the best person who ever lived, and who is the worst? Use any logical standard that's consistent. Morality, humanitarian, philanthropist—just use the same standard for both. And don't read any further until you have both names.

(Hold it! Stop! There you go again being a rebellious onion. We're halfway through the book and you're still cutting corners. I said to pick two names before you read on. You didn't do it, did you? You stink, but then being an onion you know that, don't you?)

More people choose Hitler for their worst person than any other. Saddam Hussein gave Adolf a run for his money for awhile, but he hasn't had enough time to prove himself worthy of the title of worst person ever. With your permission, we'll go with Hitler.

The best person ever is more difficult, but groups to whom I pose this question usually settle for Mother Teresa. She's a great gal. So for our purposes we'll go with her. Okay?

If you have someone else for your worst and best, use 'em. No problem. Mother Teresa would have chosen someone else. After all, the best person in the world wouldn't call herself the best. If she did, she wouldn't be.

Set up a righteousness scale.[37] Hitler is a "1" and Mother Teresa is a "9." Now, place yourself on the scale. Use your past sins as the criteria for placement. Don't choose two or three; those numbers are reserved for murderers, hit-men, dope pushers, pimps, and prostitutes. Don't be too tough on yourself—unless you are one of those.

It's important that you take the time to place yourself in comparison to the others. Do that before reading any further. And don't cheat this time.

Face it, you aren't as bad as Hitler. And you aren't as good as Mother Teresa. So how good are you? How bad have you been? What's your number?

By putting your name on the line, regardless of how good or bad a person you think you are or have been, you have admitted that some people have lived a better life than you, and some have lived worse. That's true of us all, including Mother Teresa. You have said, "In terms of being a good person, I don't measure up to some, but I'm better than others." Now, ask yourself one more question. This is the most important question asked so far, so don't go any further in the book until you answer it and understand why you responded the way you did:

Where does God draw the line when He decides who goes to heaven and who goes to hell?

Our problem is that we have been comparing ourselves with other people, instead of the perfect, holy standard of God. We might do pretty well in comparison to someone else, but we all come desperately short when we're compared to Christ. It's something like jumping the Grand Canyon with God being a "10" on the other side.

Jumping the Grand Canyon

The Grand Canyon is six miles across in most places. Let's go to a spot that's only three miles across, so we have a chance.

We're going to equate long jumping with righteousness. All you have to do to go to heaven is jump over to where God is. He's a "10" and He's on the other side, and only tens go to heaven.

Mother Teresa is first. She is the best person ever and has the best chance of reaching God on her own. So she backs up to get a good run, hikes up her habit, and takes off. At the edge she plants her take-off foot, drives up with the other leg, strains with all her might, her neck muscles tense and her leg muscles uncoil doing a double-hitch kick, and the woman soars out over the canyon—forty feet.

Incredible. Mother Teresa sets a world's record for righteousness, eclipsing the old record by over ten feet. But then, it's understandable. Talk about an adrenalin rush. Her soul is on the line. She's doing more than just jumping for her life. You'd get out there pretty good under those circumstances, too.

Where did she go?

Kerplunk. Right into the Colorado River.

Now it's Hitler's turn. He's a blob body and goes only six feet. After two bounces, where did he go?

Same place—Colorado River.

And you? How far did you get? Farther than Hitler?

Of course. But not as far as Mother Teresa. You landed somewhere in between. You ended up in the Colorado River, too.

Why?

Because we cannot reach God on our own. We're onions.

Don't get mad and accuse me of saying Mother Teresa is going to hell. I'm not. You can put any terrific person you know on the edge of the canyon. Billy Graham, Florence Nightingale, the pope, Abraham Lincoln, anyone. They'll never get across on their own merit no matter how nice they are.

But there is a fourth person on the edge. It's Jesus Christ. And He's wearing a backpack seat like parents use to carry their little kids around. Only this one has your name on it and it has been adjusted to fit your rear end. There is just one catch, and it's not the size of your posterior. You have to personally ask Him for a ride.

Your folks can't ask for you. Neither can your pastor or priest. That's why getting baptized or dedicated as a kid won't solve your hell problem. Your spouse can't ask for you, either. Neither can friends. They can pray for you, but they can't ask for you. You're the only one who can do it. And if you're too proud to ask, you don't get to go—no matter how nice you are and no matter how many wonderful things you've done.

There are some very nice people in this world who are trying to make it on their own. Others are trying to get there using the philosophies and religions dreamed up by men, women, and movies. But it looks like there is only one school of thought that God accepts. And nice people who decide not to do life God's way will spend eternity separated from Him. Why? Because nice people really do go to hell.

Chapter Seven

WHAT ABOUT THE ONES WHO NEVER HEAR? (If the whole deal is real, nice, sincere, religious people go to hell, too.)

I've led a Bible study for some years now. It's for men who are relatively new to the Bible. Most of us use the same version so we can call out page numbers. It makes it easier to turn to the passages we're studying. Men don't like to be embarrassed.

It's the kind of group where you can bring a friend and ask any question any time. Without exception, every man who is new to the Bible and the claims of Christ inquires about the same issue. And each man usually asks his question as if it was the first time anybody ever did: "What happens to the person who never hears—like the guy in the jungle, the native on an island, or the one raised in a country where Christianity isn't the mainstream religion? How can God send that person to hell? It just wouldn't be fair."

By now you know most of the answer. Onions and baseball explain a good deal of it, but not all. A deeper understanding of what's involved comes from God's general, progressive, and one-way revelations.

God's General Revelation

We'll start with Psalm 19. It contains the first half of God's general revelation:

> The heavens declare the glory of God; the skies proclaim the work of his hands. Day after day they pour forth speech; night after night they display knowledge. There is no speech or language where their voice is not heard (Psalm 19:1-3).

Go outside and look around. Not at what we have made, but at the things God has made. And don't make the mistake of looking at those parts of God's creation we have messed up. Study the result of His handiwork, not ours. Then listen.

You won't hear any words. But keep listening anyhow. A sunset screams of God. Yosemite Valley is the signature of God on the perfect canvas of creation. The Grand Canyon is His doodle after a phone conversation with Christ. Look up at the stars and tell me there is no God. You can't keep from laughing at the absurdity of the thought.

At the end of each summer, right after Labor Day, Mary and I go backpacking in the High Sierra. Usually the weather is great. The thunderstorms have ended and the snow has yet to come. Jobs and school have emptied the mountains of the masses of vacationers. It's a perfect time for hiking the trails and making a few of our own.

The last couple of years we've gone with our friends, Don and Jonie Snow. We'll spend up to ten nights on the trail. That makes our packs big and heavy.

If you've read *Counterattack*, Don is the fellow who shot the pig while he was on duty in Vietnam. It's the opening story of the book and it is hilarious. He is a retired lieutenant colonel in the army and stands five feet and six inches (I think he's fibbing. He's really not that tall). With me being six feet and eight inches, we make quite a pair.

In the evenings Don and I find the perfect campsite while the ladies rest beside the trail. (We're from the old school.) Then I set up our tent while Mary starts dinner. (She likes to cook on a camp stove.) Don and Jonie set up their tent and then help Mary with dinner while I find a good tree to keep our food safe from bears during the night. Dinner usually ends as the sun sets behind a ridge of mountains.

Last summer on the first night out, not long after the sun went down, the biggest full moon you ever saw came up, giving off enough light to read by. We couldn't believe its brilliance. So on successive nights we all guessed where the moon would show itself and sat around waiting to see who would win.

We brought no radios, telephones, televisions, or Walkmans. We brought no lanterns so when it was dark we couldn't read. And it's hard to go to sleep on those thin backpacking mats. I roll over so much I sometimes start feeling like a piece of meat on a rotisserie.

Doing nothing is a tough adjustment for us Type-A personalities. It takes me at least three days to get comfortable with nothing to do. Why is it so hard to stop doing and just be?

After dinner, my job is to find a rock facing east that's still warm from the day's sun and wide enough for all four of us to lean against. Then we get our mattresses and a sleeping bag, plop on the ground side by side, and prop up against the rock. The setting sun at our back reflects off the clouds to the east. We watch the ever-changing shapes for an hour or more, waiting for darkness. It's like a giant Rorschach ink-blot test in the evening sky. We tell each other what we see and what we think it is becoming as it changes shape; and we laugh deeply. Four people with nothing to do, enjoying each other, the evening sky—and God.

Then we play "twenty questions" until the stars appear. The person who finds the first star is praised. It is always straight up. Then we look for the second, and the third, and we keep searching until enough stars are out to make it boring. Every night we see at least one satellite arc across the sky. And every night we see at least one shooting star flame an oblique into nothingness against an ink-black background.

With no lights from the city to dim the sky, the stars are brilliant and fill the sky. City dwellers can't begin to imagine the wonder of those lights from those mountain heights. We know the North Star and the Big Dipper. And I know Orion's belt. But that's all. This year I have a star guide. Mary got it for me. I plan to learn the constellations of the summer sky. I need something to do.

The four of us sit and wait for the moon. And with its appearance and the declaration of the winner, we go to bed. The first night we were in bed by eight. The last night we were up until ten-thirty. We had watched the heavens and God had told us of Himself while we laughed and loved each other and Him.

The evening sunset and the clouds had expressed to us the reality of God. The night sky, the stars, the heavens, and the moon all gave utterance of God. And the critters prowling the campsite at night had a few things to say as well.

The day spoke just as loudly as the night. Lofty peaks, magnificent trees, petite wildflowers, deer, rock badgers, marmots, scenic vistas, and ever-changing perspectives—the expanse of His creation spoke to us, like speech itself.

But no, I haven't heard God's voice in the High Sierra. There is no speech, nor are there words; His voice is not heard. But it is felt and sensed. No rational person can deny that what we saw was the handiwork of God. The odds on Him not doing it are just too remote. It's part of God's general revelation—His attempt to show Himself to us by planting awareness in our hearts.

That makes it a lot of work to be an atheist. You have to have the Walkman of the world cranked, amped, and plugged into your ears to become deaf enough not to hear. But it can be done. There are more than a few folks who try to ignore God and explain away what He has done.

Psalm 19 is only half of God's general revelation. Romans 1 is the other half. It tells us why so many ignore the essence of the nineteenth psalm:

> The wrath of God is being revealed from heaven against all the godlessness and wickedness of men who suppress the truth by their wickedness, since what may be known about God is plain to them, because God has made it plain to them. For since the creation of the world God's invisible qualities—his eternal power and divine nature—have been clearly seen, being understood from what has been made, so that men are without excuse.
>
> For although they knew God, they neither glorified him as God nor gave thanks to him, but their thinking became futile and their foolish hearts were darkened. Although they claimed to be wise, they became fools and exchanged the glory of the immortal God for images made to look like mortal man and birds and animals and reptiles.

> Therefore God gave them over in the sinful desires of their hearts to sexual impurity for the degrading of their bodies with one another. They exchanged the truth of God for a lie, and worshiped and served created things rather than the Creator—who is forever praised. Amen (Romans 1:18-25).

The study of mankind has never revealed a society that doesn't worship. All of the remote tribes in both hemispheres have been found to revere gods and idols. Every culture in antiquity honored deities. And it is still true of communities today. We are worshiping critters. God made it so.

The heavens speak because way down deep inside our souls, God has made Himself known to us. God has revealed Himself so that on judgment day we won't be able to stand before Him and say, "But I didn't know!"

Romans 1:22 tells us that most people have claimed their own wisdom and have declared no need of God. They have become fools by worshiping themselves or things they have made, like idols and trumped-up deities.

Most people won't worship the true God, yet they end up worshiping something.

God has created an empty space inside of each person that can be filled only with Himself, no matter how hard we try to fill it with other things or ourselves. That's why it is a lot of work to be an atheist. Not only do people have to ignore what God has done around them, they also have to silence His still, small voice inside them. But that can be done. Many in Soviet leadership have done it.

Ron Carlson, the internationally known authority on cults, was speaking about the funeral of a Russian leader a few years ago. The body was being viewed. The proceedings were cold and atheistic. It was then that Chernenko's wife threw herself across his body and made the sign of a cross.[18] You can take a wife out of the country, but it's hard to take the country out of the wife. It's hard to be an atheist. His wife wasn't, and she sure didn't want her husband in hell. But her gesture didn't change a thing. At least I'd bet it didn't.

God has demonstrated Himself to all peoples of all ages through general revelation. If people respond to the awareness of God within them, it is up to God to show more. If they don't respond to general revelation, there is no need to show them more light. But if they do respond, He will amplify the revelation of Himself. I call it His progressive revelation.

God's Progressive Revelation

J. Robertson McQuilkin put it this way:

> I'd like to suggest that God's judgment is based on man's response to light received. We do not believe that men are lost for not believing in Christ when they have never heard of Christ. They are lost when they do not receive and act upon the light they have. In Luke 12:47 we read of the end time, the judgment day, when the righteousness or unrighteousness of God must stand forth, "That servant who knows his master's will and does not get ready or does not do what his master wants will be beaten with many blows." The gracious girl in Japan who, brought up in the Buddhist tradition, has been a good daughter and

> a good wife and giving to her children but has never heard of Christ is not in the same condition as the American who can turn on the television or the radio to hear the gospel any day of the week, who passes church after church on the way to the bar, but who continually rejects the light.
> Continuing Luke 12:48, "But the one who does not know and does things deserving punishment will be beaten with few blows. From everyone who has been given much, much will be demanded; and from the one who has been entrusted with much, much more will be asked."
> What is God's response to those who do receive the light? God's response to obedience is always more light.[39]

For those who respond, God will also progressively respond. He has set eternity in the hearts of men (*see* Ecclesiastes 3:11). Man continues to reach out for God. And God has not left Himself without testimony (*see* Acts 14:16-17). Those who want to find Him, can. He will continually reveal Himself to those who seek Him.

Don Richardson has written several books about the amazing biblical parallels among tribes and cultures around the world. These are evidences of God's progressive revelation. He cites tribes that have made reference to the one genuine God with names for Him that are similar to Hebrew, only there was no way they could have ever been exposed to Hebrew.[40] Others awaited a lost Book that would tell them about the God who was to be brought to them by people outside their tribe, and some of these tribes are on different continents.[41] Some tribes, whose people had never been exposed to Christianity, even had Christian symbols incorporated in their languages. For example, the Chinese symbol for *righteous* is a lamb with the letter *I* under it, meaning, "I under the lamb am righteous!" The ideograph denoting a tree is a cross with the symbol for man superimposed upon it![42] This is just a small sample of three volumes of evidence Richardson has compiled.

God has been showing Himself to the people of the world for a long time—from Adam, to Abraham, to today. And what He has revealed has been consistent. Richardson has observed a seven-component pattern in the revelation:

> 1) The fact of God's existence; 2) creation; 3) the rebellion and fall of man; 4) the need for a sacrifice to appease God and the crafty attempts of devils to make men sacrifice to them; 5) the great flood; 6) the sudden appearance of many languages and the resulting dispersion of mankind into many peoples; and finally 7) an acknowledgement of man's need of some further revelation that will seal man back into a blessed relationship with God.
>
> These seven major facts which were known before Abraham's time are still included—in a declining order of statistical occurrence—among the main components of folk religions world-wide. The degree to which any folk religion has maintained its hold on truth can be measured by how many of these seven components it still retains and with what clarity.[43]

If tribes around the world have these common components in their cultures, don't we have to conclude that God has been showing Himself? I think so. The thread of commonality is more like a huge anchor chain. If you look, you can't miss the connections. And those who respond will get even more light. But those who don't, won't.

The apostle Paul never planted a church in Athens. That Greek city was the center of intellectualism in that day. Learned men from around the world went there to share ideas. All thoughts and philosophies were welcomed. Hundreds of idols from many lands lined the streets. Any religion was okay. The only one that wasn't was the one asserting to be the only one that worked. Any person who claimed to have the only answer to any problem was run out of town—especially if the issue was what happens to you after death.

These folks respected how something was said, not necessarily what was said. If you professed your opinion with exceptional oratorical skills, it was held in high regard. Paul made his pronouncement well, but his thoughts were simply too narrow. His one-way-to-God concept just wouldn't fly. Not there, at least. So God turned off the light in Athens. No church.

It's the same today. The New Age movement says just about any ol' religion will work. They believe God is in everything and everyone, we can be our own god, and that Jesus Christ is whatever and wherever you want Him to be. The moment you remind people that lots of books have been written by men and women to tell us about God while God has written only one Book (the Bible) to tell us about Himself, they will either laugh at you or run you out of town. And for them, progressive revelation will stop.

I spoke in Germany and Spain a few years ago. What dark places spiritually! The cathedrals are colossal. The tradition is terrific. But the light has been turned off. The United States could be that way soon if we keep thinking that nice people don't go to hell.

But what about those who keep responding? God gets really specific.

The One-Way Revelation

What about other sacred books? What about those who believe the Koran instead of the Bible? What about other religions with followers outnumbering those who follow Christ? What about Eastern beliefs? What about native Americans? What about . . . ? It depends on whether the whole deal is real. Basically, it depends on God's one-way revelation.

C.S. Lewis wrote of this crucial concept in *The Chronicles of Narnia*. (They are fantastic books. Read them to your kids and grandkids. They'll enjoy them, but you'll enjoy them even more. And you all will learn a lot.)

The key players are Peter, Susan, Edmund, and Lucy. Peter and Susan are the oldest, Edmund is a liar and a sneak, and Lucy is the equivalent of Pearl Pureheart.

There is one concept Lewis develops wonderfully. He is so logical. Spock would be pleased. Let me explain his reasoning. (I'll be paraphrasing a lot now.)

The four kids are visiting an old professor in the country during the summer, and while playing hide-and-seek in the house, Lucy hides in the wardrobe closet. Nudging against the back, she finds nothing there and stumbles into the land of Narnia.

She meets some special folks and a few cool dudes and has a great time. She can hardly wait to tell her brothers and sister.

Emerging, she gathers her clan and proceeds to tell her story. Although Lucy has been a model citizen and is not known as a liar or even a stretcher of the truth, they don't believe her. The story is too far out.

That bums her out. "They don't believe me," she cries.

It's now a few weeks later and she's getting over her depression. They are playing hide-and-seek again, and once more she hides in the wardrobe closet, only this time Edmund is with her. Well, as you may have guessed, they both go into the land of Narnia. Going separate directions, Edmund meets a wicked witch and cuts a shady deal with her, promising not to tell anyone about it. Lucy has her typical great, wholesome time.

Now Lucy is really excited about telling Peter and Susan. After all, she has a witness. But Edmund lies, saying, "No, nothing like that happened. I was just humoring her."

And Peter and Susan believe Edmund.

That sends Lucy spiraling into a deeper depression. Peter and Susan get concerned and seek the old professor's advice. After telling the story, the old man asks, "Is Lucy known as a liar?"

"No sir, she always tells the truth."

"Then why don't you believe her now?" the professor replied logically. "If she has never before told a lie, it's unlikely that she would start now."

Continuing, he asks another question. "Tell me about Edmund. Is he known for telling the truth?"

"Hardly," was their combined reply. "He rarely ever tells the truth."

"Then why would you believe him now?" The professor is bewildered.

"Because the story is so far out," Peter answers, frustrated. "It's just too hard to believe. It's easier to believe Edmund."

Again the professor is logical: "I don't see what the story has to do with it at all. Why would you not believe a known truth-teller and listen to an almost pathological liar?"

Susan answers almost apologetically, "It's not that we don't believe her. It's that we think maybe . . . it could be that . . . perhaps she's . . . ."

"Crazy!" blurts the professor.

"Yes," reply the brother and sister. "Maybe she's bonkers, nutso, insane, cuckoo-bananas—you know, off her rocker. Professor, we're afraid that she might have only one oar in the water, or all her lights upstairs may not be on."

"Well, perhaps that may be true," says the professor as he considers the possibility. "Does she show any other abnormal behavior?"

"No sir; none."

"Then why would you think the girl to be mad if she hasn't shown any other signs of being off the wall?" Again the professor's logic is impeccable.

Peter and Susan are obviously frustrated. "Because sir, the story is so hard to believe."

With finality the professor ends the conversation. "It is absurd to not believe a known truth-teller, or to call her crazy, when none of her other behaviors support the thought. It is even more ridiculous to believe a known liar over someone who has always told the truth. The story has nothing to do with the issue!"

Now, that's great logic. Apply it to what Jesus said.

Jesus Christ made a statement that, if true, makes all the rest of the world's religions wrong. He does it with the one-way verse: "I am the way and the truth and the life. No one comes to the Father except through me" (John 14:6). In other words, if you want to get to God the Father, you have to go through the Son. If you want to go where God is when your physical life is over, you'll have to go through Christ. No other way will work. Jesus also made it clear that if you want to know the Father you have to know the Son, and if you don't know One you don't know the Other (*see* John 14:7-11).

C.S. Lewis concluded that Jesus was either a liar, a madman, or who He said He was—the Son of God and the Savior of mankind. A few years ago Josh McDowell made an alliteration from those conclusions by saying that Jesus was either liar, lunatic, or Lord. It's a classic argument. Let's briefly consider it.

If Jesus knew He wasn't telling the truth, that would make Him a liar and hardly someone to worship.

If He thought He was the Son of God and wasn't, that would make Him crazy and hardly worthy of worship.

There is only one other option. He is who He says He is, and that makes Him the only One to worship.

But the story is so bizarre. Is that your concern? Creation, angels, demons, heaven, hell, eternal life, God come to earth as a man, spiritual warfare—that's far out stuff. God wanting to spend forever with you, Jesus Christ wanting to serve you forever, and both wanting to have a relationship with you right now—it's so hard to believe. My friend, the story has nothing to do with it.

How do I know the whole deal is real from looking at Christ's life?

Jesus never told a lie. The record is complete enough to know. And there is no reason to believe He started telling falsehoods with the statement about Him being the only way to God. Also, none of His other behavior suggests He was crazy. The evidence shows that He led a perfect life. So there is no reason to believe He was nuts when He made His one-way statement. If the Bible is accurate, you'd have to be irrational not to believe.

Jesus Christ is God's one-way revelation. He is the only way to God.

My conclusion regarding the nice people who are on earth today is that God will prompt someone to tell them about Jesus if they respond to both God's general and progressive revelations. He did that with an Ethiopian in a chariot. God sent a man named Philip to explain the Bible to the Ethiopian (*see* Acts 8:26-39).

God will follow up on His one-way revelation today just as He did then. This book may be His method with you.

But the prime question remains unanswered: What about those who have not heard? There were people alive right after Christ died who wouldn't have had the opportunity to hear the name of Christ. What about them? And what about those in remote areas of the world today where missionaries have yet to penetrate? We still haven't resolved what happens to them. What happens if you don't get the good news about Jesus Christ? What if no one brings you the message? What happens to those who might respond if only they were told?

What about the Person Who Would Receive But Never Hears?

"Abram believed the LORD, and He credited it to him as righteousness" (Genesis 15:6). In the Old Testament, although the final sacrifice hadn't yet been provided for sin, if you believed God, you would not go to hell. The animal sacrifices performed on your behalf were an interest-only payment on your debt until Christ paid off the principal through the cross.

The word *believe* in that passage means more than intellectual agreement. It connotes coming alongside of God, alignment, commitment, and repentance. Proper biblical belief requires a change of heart. Abram had a heart for God.

In the Old Testament, the righteous (the ones who believed properly) who died went to upper Hades and awaited the event on the cross. Jesus came and took them to heaven.

How many believed God that way? Who knows? The folks of faith mentioned in the faith chapter (Hebrews 11) did. They are examples of those Old Testament righteous who believed correctly.

The chapter[44] starts off with a definition of faith: "Now faith is the assurance of things hoped for, the conviction of things not seen" (v. 1, NASB).

That is followed by a statement regarding the Old Testament faithful:

"For by it the men of old gained approval" (v. 2, NASB).

God then says in verse 3 that if you don't think He is behind the creation of the world, you might not have enough faith to get saved:

> By faith we understand that the worlds were prepared by the word of God, so that what is seen was not made out of things which are visible (NASB).

That is followed by a list of the Old Testament superstars of faith—some of the men, plus a woman, who believed God and were counted as righteous. The list includes Abel, Enoch, Noah, Abraham, Isaac, Jacob, Joseph, Moses, Rahab, Gideon, Samson, Jephthah, David, Samuel, and the prophets.

Finally, at the end of the chapter there is a statement confirming the necessity of Christ's death the cross:

> These were all commended for their faith, yet none of them received what had been promised. God had planned something better for us so that only together with us would they be made perfect (Hebrews 11:39-40).

In other words, the Old Testament righteous had to wait for Christ to die on the cross before they could get out of Hades and into heaven. Even though they hadn't heard the name of Jesus Christ they were ultimately saved by His name.

Think It Through

Do you think there might have been a person of faith living somewhere on the earth the day before Christ was crucified? Sure!

How about the day Christ died? Yes! If there was one living the day before, it is likely that the person would still be alive one day later.

How about the day after? If you said yes to the first two questions, you have to say yes to this one. But do the old rules apply even though God made a new deal when Christ did away with the law and swapped it with grace?

There certainly would not have been enough time to get the word out yet. Even while Jesus was walking around, John the Baptist was baptizing with the baptism of repentance. That's just another way of saying they believed God and it was counted to them as righteousness. John's disciples were like Abraham.

What about anyone baptized by John who died before finding out about Jesus' death? Answer: Old Testament rules applied to those who hadn't heard. If you believed God properly you were counted as righteous.

Remember, the Ten Commandments weren't given as mandates for us to keep. They were given to show how far we are from God's holiness—proof that we're onions. That's why God's commandments aren't difficult to keep . . . they're impossible!

Even though the law dominates, grace is found in the Old Testament. Remember, animal sacrifices temporarily paid the interest on our debt (sin), until Christ paid off the principal (grace). If you believed during Old Testament times, God's grace preserved your soul until Christ paid your debt.

When Christ died, grace presided over the law, but Old Testament rules still applied to those who hadn't heard. That was true for the disciples of John the Baptist.

The same rules must also apply to those who haven't heard about Jesus today.[45]

That conclusion sounds pretty logical. But something Paul said creates a problem:

> In the past God overlooked such ignorance, but now he commands all people everywhere to repent. For he has set a day when he will judge the world with justice by the man he has appointed. He has given proof of this to all men by raising him from the dead (Acts 17:30-31).

Everyone everywhere is to repent and will be judged by Christ. The proof of the appointment is the resurrection. And the phrase "all men" means *all* men (women too). Does that include those who haven't heard? Sounds like it.

Jesus said, "I am the way and the truth and the life. No one comes to the Father except through me" (John 14:6). And Peter was just as specific: "Salvation is found in no one else, for there is no other name under heaven given to men by which we must be saved" (Acts 4:12). Conclusion: Jesus is the only way into the kingdom. That's about as specific as specific can be. But are there exceptions to this rule?

It's appointed for a person to die once and then comes the judgment (*see* Hebrews 9:27). Are there exceptions? Sure! Enoch and Elijah never died. Lazarus, Jairus's daughter, the widow's son, the girl Peter raised, and the boy Elijah raised from the dead all had to die twice. The disciples raised some people to life, too. So God is perfectly capable of making exceptions to His rules. But before we get too carried away, think about this.

Scholars agree that there were at least several million people alive on the earth in the days of Noah. I don't know how many million, but living as long as they did gave them lots of time to bear lots and lots of kids. And they kept having them for hundreds and hundreds of years. They took populating the earth seriously.

Of all those millions of people, how many believed God? Take a guess. We know for sure. The Bible tells us.

Just one! Noah (*see* Genesis 6:5-9). And because of him, God let his wife and his sons and their wives live. But not because of their righteousness (they were exceptions)—only because of Noah's. And he wasn't all that righteous. He just believed God. It's important to understand the significance of this point because of the question I'm about to ask.

How many people do you think there are who haven't heard the good news about Jesus Christ, *yet* who believe God the way Abraham, Noah, and John the Baptist's disciples did?

I don't know, either. But if the hearts of those in our world bear any resemblance to the hearts of Noah's contemporaries, there aren't many. In that day there was only Noah. There may not be any today.

McQuilkin's conclusion to the question about those who haven't heard may sound like a cop-out, but I like it:

> Suppose you and I were the safety officers on the tenth floor of a condominium which cared for elderly patients. Fire broke out. We, having done our job well, knew that the official floor plan posted on the wall identified one fire escape at the end of the corridor. Perhaps it would be legitimate for me to turn over in my mind the idea that surely the architect must have put in another

> fire escape. Then, too, I remembered reading a newspaper story of someone who fell out of a tenth floor apartment and landed in a bush and survived. It might be all right for me to think of that. I'm not sure. It might be all right for me to think of tying sheets together so that some unusually strong octogenarian could climb down. But I think it would be immoral to propose such ideas in an hour like that. What do you think?
> I may not be able to prove from Scripture that no one since Calvary has ever reached heaven without a knowledge of Jesus Christ. But neither can it be proved from Scripture that anyone has done so. If it were true that people could be saved in other ways, and if it were good for people to know that, would not the Bible have told us so? Since it does not give us this hope, the hope must either be false or it must be good for people not to know about it. In either event, it would be wrong for me to speculate and propagate such an idea, because the Bible does not do so, and if it proves a false hope, what damage it would have done![46]

A story has been told about a missionary walking through the jungle who meets a man.[47] They pause on the trail to get acquainted. The man asks why the missionary has come, so the missionary tells the man about Jesus Christ.

The next words out of the native's mouth are a show stopper: "So that's His name!" He continues, "I stopped worshiping my tribe's gods to worship the three-in-one God that was revealed to me. I was to do it through the Son of that God. And until today I never knew His name. I have been persecuted greatly by my people, but I have been faithful in my worship." It appears that the man believed God, and I'll bet it was counted to him as righteousness before he heard about Christ. If the missionary had never showed up, I believe the man would have been counted like Abraham. But remember, I don't know for sure.

Can you follow the teachings of religions devised by man and be righteous? I think the first chapter of Romans says no, but what do I know? Are there exceptions? I don't think so, but for the sake of argument, allow me to say perhaps.

Can you be saved apart from the name of Jesus Christ? Peter said no. So did Jesus. But does it apply to those who never hear?

What about John the Baptist's disciples? Were there exceptions? Did God provide a loophole? Only He knows—because He'll be the One to make them. And if He does—if there are exceptions—there won't be many. Remember how many there weren't in Noah's day.

But if He doesn't make exceptions, it will be right. God is a just God, and we don't have to understand Him to make that true.

The Struggle

What about Buddhists, Hindus, and nice people in other religions who haven't heard? What about them? Dear friend, they are onions like you and me, but I think they will be judged by Old Testament law. And that's a whole lot tougher than New Testament grace. By Old Testament law you have to bat a thousand. Under New Testament grace you have to be on the right team. Which is easier to do?

Regardless of what happens to those who haven't heard, I trust my loving God to be fair. Actually, that's what I'm afraid of. I don't want Him to be fair. They'll get justice if He is. I want Him to be more than merciful, too. I want them to have eternal life, not just more time. What I really want is for God to extend grace to them. But He can't do that and be fair unless it's through Jesus Christ. So I pray for exceptions.

I don't know the probabilities of being an exception. I don't know if the odds are good or bad. What happened in Noah's day suggest bad. The loving nature of God suggest good. Does the holiness of God require justice or compassion? I just don't know, so I don't know the odds. Would you risk hell if the odds were even money? I doubt that they are that good. You wouldn't even play Russian roulette with your life on the line, let alone your soul, and those are six-to-one odds in your favor. So are you betting on being an exception? Considering the downside risk, it's just too dangerous to bet on being an exception.

Even after all this dialogue, we're still not sure what happens to the person who never hears. But what happens won't make any difference to you. You have heard. And not dealing with Christ because you don't know what's going to happen to someone else is a smoke screen. Basically, it's a cop-out. You're skirting the real issue. Don't bail out on me now. What are you going to do with Jesus Christ?

Who Do You Say That He Is?

God sent Christ to communicate the depth of His love for us and to show how far from God we have strayed. Jesus is the only solution to the problem of sin (the stuff that separates us from God). God wants us to know about His Son. And once He has shown Christ to you, the next move is yours.

God's one-way revelation requires a response. Remember what Peter said. He had the right answer. We talked about it back in chapter four:

> Once when Jesus was praying in private and his disciples were with him, he asked them, "Who do the crowds say I am?"
> They replied, "Some say John the Baptist; others say Elijah; and still others, that one of the prophets of long ago has come back to life."
> "But what about you?" he asked. "Who do you say I am?"
> Peter answered, "The Christ of God" (Luke 9:18-20).

There are a lot of things being said about Jesus Christ. In some circles He is a swear word. In New Age circles He's anything, anyone, and everywhere. In public schools He's a no-no. But God is not concerned with groups. He wants individual relationships. "What about you? Who do you say that He is?"

Peter's answer was the equivalent of saying "My personal Savior." He had responded properly to God's one-way revelation.

God gave you His general revelation. If you respond to it He'll show you His progressive revelation. If you respond to that you'll get His one-way revelation. And if you respond to it, you'll become a child of God. That's winning big time.

Chapter Eight

WHAT WOULD YOU PAY FOR A SOUL? (If the whole deal is real, there is nothing more valuable than a soul.)

In the military, when going on patrol, one person is put out front, ahead of the rest. His job is to sense danger in order to protect the rest of the squad. If he gets shot, at least the rest won't get ambushed. They lose a lot of scouts, but it saves a lot of lives in the long run. Destroyers are risked to protect aircraft carriers. Secret-service agents are trained to jump between an assassin's bullet and the President for the good of the country. We actually watched a man do that for President Reagan on national TV some years ago. First Officer Spock chose to die to save the *Enterprise* in a *Star Trek* movie. We see people risk their lives all the time on "Rescue 911" and other similar TV shows. Why do we do such things?

There is a principle at work. Military generals use this principle in decision making all the time. If the giving or taking of a comparatively few lives now will save more lives later, it's a good thing to do. During World War II the United States dropped two atomic bombs on Japan using this same logic.

The principle can be learned from the movie *Star Trek II*. As I mentioned, First Officer Spock, a Vulcan, willingly gives his life to save the ship. His reasoning is a statement of the principle, When it comes to life and death the needs of the many outweigh the needs of the few or the one. It's the formula by which heroes are made.

But in *Star Trek III*, a new principle is introduced. (By the way, it would make the devout humanist creator of the "Star Trek" series, Gene Roddenberry, roll over in his grave if he knew I was making a Christian application of his work.) Kirk and his friends risk their careers, court martial, jail, and their lives to get Spock out of hell (that's possible with Vulcans). Their reasoning: The needs of the one outweigh the needs of the many. That's when I had a classic *Aha!* experience. It hit me like a ton of bricks. I finally understood the parable of the ninety-nine sheep and one:

> Suppose one of you has a hundred sheep and loses one of them. Does he not leave the ninety-nine in the open country and go after the lost sheep until he finds it? And when he finds it, he joyfully puts it on his shoulders and goes home. Then he calls his friends and neighbors together and says, "Rejoice with me; I have found my lost sheep." I tell you that in the same way there will be more rejoicing in heaven over one sinner who repents than over ninety-nine righteous persons who do not need to repent (Luke 15:4-7).

I had never understood why a responsible shepherd would put a whole herd at risk for one lousy sheep that didn't have sense enough to come in out of the rain. Don't waste your time looking for the lost one—not if it puts the herd at risk. Rustlers and coyotes could have a field day with a herd left unattended. Maybe the stray will wander back, maybe not. Why gamble? The downside risk is too great for such a small upside potential. At least you still have ninety-nine.

But that's not the way God sees it. Not then, not now. God doesn't view the loss of the herd as downside risk at all. And He sees the upside as having the maximum return possible. Paul explained it this way:

> I eagerly expect and hope that I will in no way be ashamed, but will have sufficient courage so that now as always Christ will be exalted in my body, whether by life or by death. For to me, to live is Christ and to die is gain. If I am to go on living in the body, this will mean fruitful labor for me. Yet what shall I choose? I do not know! I am torn between the two: I desire to depart and be with Christ, which is better by far; but it is more necessary for you that I remain in the body (Philippians 1:20-24).

What's the worst thing that can be done to a Christian? Kill him! But dying is a good thing because he will go to heaven. That was Paul's attitude, and it eliminated the downside risk.

The apostle said he was ready to die because he would really like to be with his heavenly Father. But for the sake of the believers, he would be content to live and continue ministering. He wins if he dies, and he wins if he lives. Not having a downside risk gave him a great outlook and total freedom. He didn't own anything, so there was nothing to lose. And he didn't even own his life anymore. Paul had given himself to the Lord. He had no downside risks at all.

Likewise, there is no risk when the shepherd leaves the herd. The ninety-nine sheep were saved sheep and represent Christians. You can't do much to them. What matters is saving the lost one . . . even at the risk of losing part or all of the herd.

Give one life to save several lives. That makes sense. But to give many lives whose souls are saved in order to save one lost soul makes even more sense. You see, the bigger issue is the soul, not the life.

Life is temporal. A soul lasts forever. It's easy to see which is more important. A soul has the greater value.

What would you pay for a soul? You're a bettin' kinda' guy or gal, aren't you? What would you risk?

Don't answer yet. You don't have enough information to decide. Before you can understand the value of a soul, you need to know what a life is worth.

The Rising Cost of Living

Environmental safety programs provide guidelines to the value of life. So do insurance companies and lawsuits. What we'll spend to save lives in the workplace and what we're worth to our heirs in settlements after death will help establish our worth.

Our body chemicals were worth a total of $7.28 in 1985.[48] (In that regard, I am probably worth more than you are. I'm six-foot eight and weigh 225 pounds.) Life must be worth the difference between the value of our elements and what we are willing to spend to save it. Or, life must be worth what we are willing to pay to compensate for its loss.

In America, one way of determining the value of life is by calculating the number of work-related deaths recorded over a period of time, assessing the amount of money spent to improve the work environment or add safeguards on a job site, and then remeasuring work-related deaths over the same period of time. Divide the number of lives saved into the amount spent and we have the value of a life. Work-safety officials are currently spending as much as $3.5 million per life saved. And the Environmental Protection Agency is spending from $400,000 to $7 million per life saved, depending on the program.[49]

An insurance group put a housewife's value at $1.4 million to show that she needed life insurance.[50] Some executives have been worth as much as $7 million to their companies after courtroom litigation. In 1979, families of plane-crash victims averaged more than $500,000 in court-awarded compensation. That number is currently in the $350,000 range. We're not worth as much now if we crash in an airplane as we were if we had bought the farm in a plane ten years ago. Inflation has not increased the value of plane-crash victims.

There have been times in history when life wasn't worth much. Slavery, attempts to exterminate races, refusal to help starving masses, man's cruelty to the poor and underprivileged, sweat shops, snuff films, porn flicks, and abuse of children all demonstrate a low value of life. Baby girls in China have less value than baby boys. With the size of families being regulated, parents of girls will often kill their daughters until they have a boy. Life had little value in Cambodia during the "killing fields" years, and isn't worth much today in famine-stricken Africa. But it's worth up to $7 million in the United States if your earnings are up there.

Strangely, the threat of death is sometimes worth more than the loss of life. As we have seen, a life is worth as much as $7 million. But the threat of death is worth $21 million. That was the amount awarded to a man who was exposed to AIDS, but didn't get the disease. The courts must have figured that living with Rock Hudson was worse than dying. After the opposition appealed, the final settlement was still more than $3 million dollars.

Are folks from different walks of life worth more than others? Are people who die one way worth more than if they die another? Is life in one country worth more than in another?

It looks like it.

Does that mean life is like any other commodity that swings in value according to market conditions?

Yes! There are variables in man's determination of the worth of life. Let's look at a few of them.

Supply and Demand

In economics, value is primarily determined by supply and demand. The greater the supply, the less a commodity is worth. The greater the demand, the more people will pay for it. We value gold because it's pretty and rare. It's the same with diamonds. Other precious stones aren't perceived as being as attractive as diamonds. And other gems are easier to obtain. Diamonds are tough to find. The result: diamonds have greater value than other precious gems. Supply and demand dictate worth.

The same principles tend to apply to the value of life. Life isn't as precious in China and India. There are so many people, life has been devalued. Couple that with widespread poverty and disease, then add a fatalistic religion, and life's value diminishes further. Rats and cows are just as valuable as people in India. Starvation in Ethiopia and death in Haiti is commonplace. Death has little meaning and life has little value in those places. We become immune because the masses involved are so great. Huge numbers make life impersonal.

But strand a few whales in the ice pack in the Arctic, call attention to the situation with television coverage, and we'll spend millions to save them. Saving a few starving people when there are so many isn't news. But apparently saving a few whales when there are so few is. Does that make whales more valuable than people?

For some people, a pet is worth more than a starving child. We have a cat named Stephanie. For what it costs to feed her each month, we could feed a starving child through Compassion International (we do) or World Vision. What does that say about our values? We have but one cat, and we're attached. We don't know any of the millions of starving kids.

This whole concept is getting scary. But you ain't heard nothin' yet.

How Much Does It Cost?

Supply and demand is one criterion for establishing value. Cost effectiveness is another. Try this on for size:

> Researchers from Brown University and a Rhode Island hospital did a cost-benefits analysis of treating handicapped infants. The answer: For birth weights of less than 900 grams, or about 2 pounds, costs per survivor exceeded the child's potential average lifetime earnings. Rescuing heavier babies returned more than the expense to society.[51]

Some people are suggesting that we make a person's earning potential the guideline for saving his or her life. Life-and-death decisions could be made on the basis of cost effectiveness.

Don't be shocked. People are already doing that now in other ways. Some abortions are performed for economic reasons. If a mother can't afford a kid she can kill it, as long as it's in the womb. If she waits a day until the kid is in a crib, it's called murder. What a difference a day makes.

But we ain't seen nothin' yet. Older people will be the next to go. There will be so many, and the economic drain will be extreme. Just watch. We'll change the laws to make it easy to kill them. And those suffering from AIDS will follow. It takes so long to die from the disease, and the medical costs are shooting off the charts. We'll figure some way to kill them. You'll see.

The combined cost of caring for a burgeoning elderly population and a geometric increase of AIDS patients will break the medical bank of any country that attempts to deal with the problems humanely. Therefore, a decision to kill the dying will occur. It's inevitable. Once we opened the door to legalized murder on the basis of economics, like we did for abortion, we also opened it to kill any group that becomes too costly to maintain. Life has become a cost issue.

As we have seen, our society values life on the basis of supply and demand and cost effectiveness. People also value other people on the basis of relationship, how good or bad they've been, and their potential and productivity.

Relationship

If you're a high-school student, consider this startling and frightening statistic. (If you're a parent, you'll be shocked.)

A denomination did a study on the high-school graduates from their Sunday schools. Two years after high-school graduation, only 4 percent remained active in their faith. Further, only 30 percent of the 96 percent who fell away ever came back to the organized church. The numbers were so bad the denomination decided not to publish the results. That's why the source is private.

The morning my son John went away to the University of California at Berkeley on a basketball scholarship I wrote the following article for my monthly newsletter, "Obedient Thoughts." I had to leave for Chicago to speak at a church. My son would leave for college before I returned.

I felt a lot like Abraham as I left because I knew about the 4-percent study I mentioned earlier. I tell this story as if I heard it from someone else, but don't be fooled. I portrayed myself as Jabraham, my son is Jonssac—and my heart was heavy.

> I recently heard a story about Jabraham and Jonssac. Let me tell you the tale.
>
> Jabraham lived with his family in the northwest part of his world. He had been chosen by God to preach and the Lord had blessed the man with a wonderful wife and two terrific children, the younger being a son whose name was Jonssac.
>
> In those days the inhabitants of the land loved their sports. One of the favorites was hucking honeydew melons through hula hoops attached to the side of huts.
>
> Jonssac was the best honeydew hucker for his age in the land. He was so good in fact that he earned the right to go huck honeydews for Honeydew U. Jabraham was pleased because that

saved him 75,000 gourds. (That's how much it cost to go to Honeydew U. for five years when you were from the northwest.)

I might add that old Jabraham had been regarded as a pretty good honeydew hucker in his day. But now he was old and could no longer keep up with the young hucksters. God had been gracious though and had allowed the old man the strength to hoop honeydews while Jonssac had been in high school. Playing with his son had fulfilled a lifetime dream for the father. Jabraham thought his son had enjoyed it too. As a matter of fact, even though Jonssac was the player of the year in the territory, an All-American, had played against the Russialakites, and had made the Jr. Olympics final four, the boy's greatest moment in sports came when he finally beat his dad at the beginning of his last year in high school. What fun those two had together.

The days had been glorious for the patriarch. Few there are who get to huck with their son after the son has grown bigger and runs faster. But now that those times were past, Jabraham had given up hucking honeydews with an air of satisfaction. He was content with the past. But the old man had two great concerns about the future. One was selfish.

The old hobbled huckster was losing his playmate and he was sad. Although the boy had become a man, the dad and the son were pals. They had done more than huck honeydews together. Many a night they had polished off a large manna pizza together watching "Late Night With a Lettermakite" after the boy returned from a time with a lass. Yes, the father would miss the boy—more than he ever dreamed. You see, God had given the boy to the old man eighteen years before, but now wanted him back. And to make matters worse for the dad, Honeydew U. was located very close to Gomorrahville. The dad was reluctant to give the boy back, and he was scared to death to let him go to sin city.

Jabraham knew the percentages. The bookmaker, Jimmy the Jew, had always set the odds on the honeydew games. That's why the old man knew the odds on his son staying true to the God of his father. Jonssac had a 4 percent chance. That's right, there was only a 4 percent chance of survival. Only four out of a hundred continued in the faith after two years away from home during their "U" years, and only 30 percent who drifted away ever came back later on in life. Jabraham had a right to be scared. No wonder he didn't want to let him go. How could he sacrifice him to the suburbs of Gomorrahville—the dreaded city of Soderbia? But he had to; it was time. He had no choice anyhow. His boy was his own man.

The old man woke up on a Saturday. It was a morning he had long dreaded. This particular morning Jabraham had to take a winged chariot to the land of Chicagolon and would be gone a week. On the following Thursday his man-child would depart for Honeydew U. His beloved son would be gone when he returned home.

The good-bye was kept short that morning, but Jonssac knew of the pain his father was suffering. It was in the old man's voice when he paused at

> the door and called back that final time. The boy knew the patriarch would be wiping his eyes as he got into his land chariot. He was right, but what he didn't know was that Jabraham continued to wipe them for over twenty leagues. As a matter of fact, he had to wipe them frequently as he told me this story.
>
> After he finished telling me his tale in the chariot-port, where he was waiting for his flight, the last thing I heard Jabraham say was a prayer. "God," he pleaded, "please send a ram for a substitute sacrifice. I can't find one in the thicket. If you don't, please surround my son with your warring angels that he might overcome the odds and be a 'four percenter.'"

My deepest, most fervent, and aggressive prayers have been for my children. I will continue praying passionately for them. I have prayed that God would make them "four percenters." Mary and I have been given two great gifts from the Lord. Our son is studying to be a family counselor and our daughter is heading for the mission field.

Do you get an idea of how valuable my kids are to me? My offspring are more important to me than yours are. Aren't yours more important to you than mine? Sure. And I pray for mine more than I pray for yours. You, too, for yours? You bet! If you are a young person, your dad is more important to you than I am. That's the way it is with loved ones.

Let's say you've just jumped into a burning school bus. You have two arms to grab two kids and run before it blows. No second trips. Your son and daughter are in the second row. How do you choose who to take?

Wouldn't you bypass those in the front seats to get to your kids? I would, too.

Loved ones are worth more to us than people we don't know. So are good friends and some relatives.

I remember a movie where in the early stages of the story a junior-high boy was hassling his younger elementary-school-aged sister. They didn't seem to like each other much.

A bit later the boy stepped off a curb and was hit by a car. At the hospital the doctors told the parents a transfusion was needed. But his blood type was rare and they didn't have any in stock. However, they thought the sister might be the same type. The parents confirmed it—she was.

The mother asked her daughter if she would give blood to save her brother's life. To the mother's surprise, she didn't say yes. She wanted to think about it.

A few minutes later, the girl returned and told her folks she had decided to give the necessary transfusion and was ready. The next scene showed the girl lying on a gurney, wired to her brother in the emergency room. Red liquid filled the tubes connecting them.

A perplexed look came upon the little girl's face. She was confused as she spoke. "When do I die?" she asked.

"What?" replied her startled mother.

"I want to know, Mommy. When do I die?"

The mom looked at her husband and realized what was going through her daughter's mind and understood why she needed some time to consider the transfusion. The little girl thought she had to die to save her brother's life.

We tend to value life more when it's personal. That's why I have a cat. I've never seen the faces of the starving masses up close and personal.

Short-term missions are wonderful for changing perspectives. The organizers hope the missionary won't mess up anything too much. And they don't expect much from the workers. Let's face it, their contribution is usually minimal. But a short-term experience in a third-world environment makes the missionary get personal with the people, and a person is rarely ever the same after that. I guess a trip to a mission field might even be cause to get rid of your cat when you get back.

Over the years I've asked people what their criteria would be if they were in a position to spend their money to save a life. In my informal study, relationship has been the most important criterion for establishing value. The second most mentioned-prioritizing factor pertained to the kind of sin committed. Or, stated in another way, how good or bad has the person been in comparison with others?

Kind of Sin (How Good or Bad?)

If I'm going to spend some money, I want my dollars to count. Nobody likes a bad investment. That's why most people would rather spend their money on someone who is perceived to be a good person than on someone bad. I'd spend my money to save a white-collar criminal before I would a murderer, wouldn't you? Give me a teller of lies over the night stalker any day. These days adulterers aren't considered criminals, so most people (including me) would spend their money faster for them than they would a rapist. Who would you choose between a skid-row alcoholic or a Hell's Angel biker? I'd spend my money on the drunk.

Then there are some of us who would rather just keep the money. I'm not interested in saving a serial killer who has no conscience. Let him burn. I could use a new car. I don't want to spend any money on a non-repentant, chronic child molester. I'm afraid he'll do it again. Let him burn, too. Baby needs a new pair of shoes! Are there circumstances that would cause me to value money over lives? It looks like it. And I'm embarrassed as I write.

In addition to these variables, there are two more that I'd like to discuss briefly. The first is potential and productivity. The second is religion.

Potential and Productivity

If the amount of money I have to spend on rescuing souls is fixed, I want to get as much bang for my buck as I can. I like a bargain. So I think I would spend my money on someone who, in addition to being a good person, would also do the most good.

Let's assume I have a fixed amount of money. With it I can save the life of one more person. My choice must be made between you and the next Billy Graham. Guess what? Burn, baby, burn. Tough break. You're charcoal.

Wouldn't you spend more on Mother Teresa than some scum-bag puke of a Hell's Angel? Me, too. And most would spend more on a young person who has his whole life in front of him than on an older person who has left most of his life behind. Wouldn't you spend more on a healthy baby than one with defects—unless it was yours, or unless the old person was your mom or dad?

One person I asked said she would spend her money on a rich person under the condition that all the saved person's money be used to save other lives. That sounded creative, but it's conditional. But then, that's what all the other variables are as well.

Religion

As I said, rats, cows, and humans all have the same value to a Hindu. That rat might be your uncle. The cow might be an aunt. Suffering is considered part of perfecting a person for his next life, so no one wants to help. Pain is seen as God's will. Thus, fatalistic religions devalue life.

Ron Carlson mentioned that during wars and after catastrophes you rarely see Hindus, Moslems, or Buddhists caring for their fellow Hindus, Moslems, or Buddhists. The group you'll see helping is the Red Cross.[52]

The red in the cross represents the blood of Christ. The cross represents how He died and why. And that symbol is recognized internationally as the sign of compassion and caring.

Life is held in high esteem where Christianity has left its mark.

Life has little value, except to loved ones, where Jesus is not honored.

We have to conclude that the value of life depends on a multiple of variables. Supply and demand in the marketplace is one of them. Cost effectiveness, relationship, how good or bad, potential and productivity, and religion are others. The value of life certainly varies culturally as well.

These are a few of the variables that determine the value of a life. But what about a soul? Do the same variations in value apply?

The Value of a Soul

I was to speak at a fundraising banquet for a Christian conference center near Seattle. The event usually raised a few thousand dollars. Most of the attendees were businessmen.

Having an angle can be helpful, so I inquired about the money needed and its use. They wanted to raise $22,000 to winterize some cabins for year-round occupancy. Attendance at the conference center would be increased by 550 people per year if they could gather the money.

I asked about the percentage of people who attended the center that made professions of faith. I was told the number was around 10 percent. Having a calculating mind, I quickly determined that fifty-five souls would be added to the kingdom each year for an investment of $22,000. That's four hundred dollars a soul. Amortized over a ten-year period, the cost would be reduced to forty dollars per soul. That sounded like a good deal to me and I thought it would play well, so I pitched it hard.

"How many of you would pay five thousand dollars for a soul if you knew the money would keep someone from hell, or if it would snatch someone out?" I asked boldly. A couple of heads nodded. I knew I was in.

"How about twenty-five hundred?" was my next entrapment.

The audience was wary. But a couple of more heads nodded. *Duck soup!* I thought.

"How about a grand, and you would know for certain that a soul was rescued from hell? Would you pay a thousand dollars for a soul? That would be a good deal, wouldn't it?" I tried to push them into agreement. They relaxed and it looked like they were going for it.

"If we could cut a deal with the devil, suppose he was willing to sell souls for five hundred dollars. Kinda' like a one-day-no-bake sale. How many would you pop for?" I was leading them down the path. Carty, the manipulator, was at work.

"Would I have more takers at four hundred dollars?"

"Of course," was their response.

"What if the price came down to four hundred dollars, but that one-time investment would be good each year for ten years thereafter, thus getting your per soul cost to forty dollars? Do you think you would value a soul sufficiently to make a four hundred dollars investment right now?"

With that question I had 'em. They had forgotten about the banquet and why they had been invited. They were into the concept. The bottom-line approach to the value of a soul had disarmed them. They were putty in my hands. I applied the close.

"That's exactly what you can do tonight. Although you won't specifically know the person saved, based on past performance, a gift of four hundred dollars tonight will produce ten saved souls in the next ten years. It's no longer hypothetical. Put your money where your mouth is. Give the dollars necessary to winterize these cabins." With that I sat down.

Fifteen thousand dollars was given that night. The camp people would have been happy with their usual three thousand. But I was disappointed. They were only willing to pay $273 a soul.

Remember the variables by which we determine the value of life: supply and demand, economics, relationship, how good or bad, potential and productivity, and religion. We use the same variables to determine the value of a soul, but an element of belief must be thrown in or we won't spend as much.

If you are in a burning car and I know you're about to lose your life, I'll probably react to save you. But I can't see your soul. And I don't know if you are going to hell, even if there is such a place. I've never seen it. And you are such a nice person I can't imagine you would end up there anyhow. The result is that I won't risk as much because I'm not sure of your outcome. In the burning car I know you're probably going to die. I don't know if you are going to hell. If I'm going to risk something, it's easier to do it if I'm sure of the consequences. That's why I tend to risk more to save a life than a soul.

This soul business requires an element of faith not required in issues of life and death. That's why most people will pay more for a life than a soul. Most people don't believe the Bible.

We don't believe that nice people really do go to hell, so we're not willing to risk as much to save them.

A life is tangible and its loss directly affects me. A soul is an intangible and its loss affects God. Most people care more about themselves than God, so they care more about lives than souls.

Let's look at the variables and the value of a soul from God's perspective. I think you'll find it enlightening. Our ways really are different from His ways and our hearts are dissimilar indeed. We'll start by grouping the first three variables.

Supply and Demand, Economics, and Relationship

Are you worth less to God if you live in an overpopulated country?

Are you worth less if you are among the thousands who are starving?

Is your worth established by your economic contribution or cost?

Is your worth based upon your closeness to God?

Is your worth to God established by your circumstances or something you do or don't do?

Does Jesus sort out our value according to man's variables? Absolutely not! Does He play favorites, like we do? Not on your life! Perhaps I should say, "Not on your soul!" Matthew offers proof positive.

> While He was still speaking to the multitudes, behold, His mother and brothers were standing outside, seeking to speak to Him. And someone said to Him, "Behold, Your mother and Your brothers are standing outside seeking to speak to You." But He answered the one who was telling Him and said, "Who is My mother and who are My brothers?" And stretching out His hand toward His disciples, He said, "Behold, My mother and My brothers! For whoever shall do the will of My Father who is in heaven, he is My brother and sister and mother" (Matthew 12:46-50, NASB).

Jesus made two very important points in this passage. The first pertains to our relationship with Him.

His critics thought He had just put down His mom.

"Mother hater! Mother hater! Jesus hates His mother," said His detractors.

But what He had just said was that blood-line relationships, as important as they are, end with the cessation of life. Spiritual relationships, on the other hand, last for all eternity, making them far more important.

Jesus had also just said something about love. "God is love; you understand that," He would say if He were explaining it today. "And I am God the flesh. Since God loves perfectly, I too love perfectly. I can love only the way God loves, because that's who I am. That makes Me incapable of loving in degrees. Therefore, I cannot love My mother any more than I love you, nor you any more than My mother."

What an unbelievable revelation.

Jesus loves you just as much as He loves His mom.

WOW! No matter how unlovely you think you are, Jesus loves you as much as He does His mother. Your image of yourself doesn't alter His love for you one whit. If you are one of His partakers (I don't like the word follower; too many are too many steps behind Him), you will not take your trip into the kingdom in coach or in the back of the bus. Those who know Him will go first class all the way, regardless of their lot in life. There is no caste system in the kingdom. You're probably surprised at the realization that God loves us all the same. I was. But it is impossible for Him to love any other way.

Love is one thing, worth or value is quite another. How is our worth determined? The answer: by God's love. Apart from Him loving us, we have no eternal value. Don't ever forget that you're an onion. You stink. Work as hard as you want at being good and you're still an onion—you just won't smell quite as bad. So as onions, what are we worth? Nothing, if we're looking at ourselves. Onions don't have much value. But we humans don't like to think of ourselves as worthless, so we try to make a silk purse out of an onion skin.

Man has a tendency to put himself at the center of the universe. With our inflated value of ourselves we try to make everything revolve around us. But it's supposed to revolve around God.

Sin is attempting to make ourselves like God. Satan started it; we just continued the process. Therefore we try to see ourselves as being worth what God has done for us (sending Jesus Christ to die on our behalf). We tend to think that what Christ did demonstrates how valuable we are.

And we are valuable—but not because of what we've done or who we are. We are valuable because God loves us. Period! In and of ourselves we do not have worth. Consider the following passage as evidence:

> You see, at just the right time, when we were still powerless, Christ died *for the ungodly*. Very rarely will anyone die for a righteous man, though for a good man someone might possibly dare to die. But God demonstrates his own love for us in this: *While we were still sinners*, Christ died for us (Romans 5:6-8, emphasis added).

Are we worth the death of God's Son? Did God get a good deal when He swapped Jesus for us? Consider Steve Halliday's answer to the question (Steve is my editor):

> If so, then grace is no more grace, for God was only pursuing a good bargain. Grace, on the other hand, says that although we were "worth" nothing—in fact, we deserved all the horrors of hell—God, in His unfathomable love, decided to save us anyway and make us into something beautiful that would display His own matchless glory before the watching universe. Our salvation is based on God's worth, not our own.

God said the same thing to the Jews who thought they were a big deal because of who they were, rather than because of who God is:

> The LORD did not set his affection on you and choose you because you were more numerous than other peoples, for you were the fewest of all peoples. But it was because the LORD loved you and kept the oath he swore to your forefathers that he brought you out with a mighty hand and redeemed you from the land of slavery, from the power of Pharaoh king of Egypt (Deuteronomy 7:7-8).

I think Steve's assessment of this passage is right on: "In other words, Israel, God loved you because He loved you, not because you were "worth" it. The same is true with us."

So what's your soul worth? What is its value? Well, let me tell you one thing. Your value has not been established by the variables of man. It doesn't vary according to market conditions. And it's certainly not based on intrinsic value. You're an onion.

As a matter of fact, there are no variables determining your worth from God's perspective. "For it is by grace you have been saved, through faith—and this is not from yourselves, it is the gift of God—not by works, so that no one can boast" (Ephesians 2:8-9). One act, and only one, determined the value of your soul. Your soul is worth whatever the life of God's Son is worth to the Father Himself—but only because He loves you. And because of His unconditional love, nothing else in creation approaches your kind of value.

God's love makes your soul the most valuable entity in the universe.

A final word about market variables needs to be said. Neither supply and demand nor economics are factored into your value to the Lord. And neither God nor Jesus loves in degrees. They do not value one person over another. So in that regard, relationship is not an issue. But relationship is an issue in that you must know Jesus Christ personally. His love for you won't alter, whether or not you enter into a relationship with Him. His love for you isn't conditional. But the forgiveness of your sin is. You must have a relationship with Jesus Christ or you will receive the justice your sin demands.

Kind of Sin (How Good or Bad?)

How would Jesus spend His money? No! I must rephrase that question. How did Jesus spend Himself?

For what sins did Jesus not die? Are any iniquities not covered under the atoning "handiwrap" of His blood? Let's take a look.

How about adultery?

No, that one's covered. The woman at the well (*see* John 4:1-42) and the woman at the temple (*see* John 8:1-11) are good examples of Christ forgiving adulterers.

Did He die for thieves and robbers?

Look no further than the man hanging on the cross next to our Lord.

How about murder?

"But God demonstrates His own love toward us, in that while we were yet sinners, Christ died for us" (Romans 5:8, NASB). Is that an all-inclusive statement? You bet. Does the word *sinners* mean some sinners or all sinners? All sinners means all sinners, including repentant murderers. Paul made that crystal clear:

> Do you not know that the wicked will not inherit the kingdom of God? . . . And that is what some

> of you were. But you were washed, you were sanctified, you were justified in the name of the Lord Jesus Christ and by the Spirit of our God (1 Corinthians 6:9,11).

King David is a child of God and he murdered. That means Jesus' death applied to his sin. Repentant murderers are covered by the blood of Christ.

What about suicide?

Suicide is a form of murder, so it's covered. If good works can't save you, then bad works, including suicide, can't cost you your salvation.

So Jesus Christ did die for all sin. But do you have to ask forgiveness for each sin you've committed to have it forgiven?

Certainly not! The believer who committed a sin and died before praying about it died with the Spirit of God grieved and quenched. He died miserable with no fruit of the Spirit evident, but he died in Christ. He left this world not experiencing love, joy, peace, patience, kindness, goodness, faithfulness, gentleness, and self-control, but he went to be with the Father.

Blasphemy against the Holy Spirit (*see* Matthew 12:31) is an unforgivable sin. What about that one?

Some people who have cursed God in moments of anger and remorse worry that they have done it. But they haven't. That's not what blasphemy against the Holy Spirit is. Some people worry they may have committed the unforgivable sin sometime during their life. Not possible. Your desire to be with the Father is evidence of your salvation, if you know Christ. Jesus died for every person who ever cursed Him.

I like what one seminary prof says: This could be called the "unrepentable sin" rather than the unforgivable sin, since no one who commits it would ever want to repent of it. God would never lead a person to repentance, then say, "Ha-ha on you! You'd like to be forgiven, but I'm not gonna' do it!" In other words, if you're worried you've committed it, you couldn't have.

Blasphemy against the Holy Spirit is defined as attributing the miracles of Jesus to the power of satan. It's the ultimate conduct of a hardened heart. But since Jesus isn't walking this earth in human form now, most theologians don't believe it's possible to commit this sin any more. I agree with them. That's not one you have to worry about doing.

The Bible talks about the sin unto death in 1 John 5:16-17. Can people who do that one be saved?

Sure. The sin unto death involves the believer who is getting in the way of something God wants to do, so the Father takes him or her out of the picture and brings that person home to heaven. My mom is an example. Having been an alcoholic for years, she received Christ in her mid-sixties. She was relatively dry for several years, then started to slip again. It was like God said, "Let's not go through that drill again. Come on home." He laid her down on the sofa and took her to Himself. I believe she committed the sin unto death.

Does the number of times you've messed up matter?

Peter was trying to be a big shot in front of Jesus. The law required a Jew to forgive three times. So Peter was showing off when he asked Jesus, "How many times should I forgive? Seven?" (*see* Matthew 18:21).

Jesus made him blink twice, drop back, and punt when He said, "Seventy times seven." In other words, beyond all reasonable numbers.

How many times will He forgive you if you have a repentant heart?

Seventy times seven? An unlimited number, if you are repentant when you come to Him.

However, if you persist with your sin you do have to consider whether you were saved in the first place. One who practices sin is lost (*see* 1 John 3:8-9).

The bottom line is: 1) If you don't know Jesus there is no forgiveness of sin; 2) If you do know Jesus, forgiveness for sin restores your relationship with the Holy Spirit. Think of the Holy Spirit as your power source. He's the engine. Sin powers down the engine. Forgiveness powers it up. The engine is always there. It's just not always turned on. And as a forgiven believer you can again demonstrate the fruit of the Spirit. (By now you should remember what that fruit consists of: love, joy, peace, patience, kindness, goodness, faithfulness, gentleness, and self-control.)

Don't forget, as a believer forgiveness is yours as often as you need it. It's bottomless and never runs out. However, you also need to remember that you're not getting away with anything. Sin is costly. Oh, it's pleasurable for a season. If sin wasn't fun, nobody would do it. Unfortunately, it always leaves you down and deeply scarred. Getting a scar and living without the fruit is a bad trade.

The bottom line is that just as Jesus doesn't play favorites among those who know Him, neither does our past get in the way of our personal relationship with Him. That's good news. And I have more good news. He doesn't favor high-potential producers over the rest of us either. He loves you and me just as much as He loves Billy Graham or Mother Teresa.

Potential and Productivity

Jesus mentioned five special groups that need a break and will get special treatment from Him in heaven. When we minister to them it is as if we are ministering to Christ Himself (*see* Matthew 25:35-40). They are widows, orphans, the sick and afflicted, the poor, and people in prison for Christ's sake. That's a low-potential group of folks who don't have much going for them.

Let me illustrate how potential and productivity bias my values. I lead a nonprofit organization called "Yes! Ministries." My motto is, "Helping people say yes to God." To live and minister, I am dependent on support from other believers. With that in mind, which of the following gifts do you think I would prefer?

A man with a million dollars gives me a gift of one-hundred thousand dollars.

A man with a thousand dollars gives me five hundred dollars.

A widow with a penny gives me a penny.

Hey, I'm no fool. I'll take the hundred grand.

Which is the greater gift?

Don't try to get spiritual with me. A hundred G's is worth a whole bunch more to me than a penny. But God's value system is different. Again, our ways aren't the same.

God is not interested in amounts. All He wants is everything you have, everything you will have, everything you are, and everything you will be. That's all. And who gave Him all? The widow. The millionaire gave 10 percent. The middle guy gave fifty percent. But the widow gave 100 percent. The amount didn't matter to God. Therefore, the widow gave the greatest gift (*see* Mark 12:41-43).

We all have time, talent, and treasure. And each of us has 100 percent of whatever has been entrusted to us. What we do with our 100 percent is what matters. That means we're all in the same boat and we're all the same in God's eyes. Potential and productivity are variables that are important only to man, not God. High rollers for the kingdom aren't favored by the Father. Isn't that good news for you and me?

We've seen how most of the value variables affect the worth of a soul. Another important one remains to be discussed.

Religion

Individuals in the fatalistic religions—like Hindus, Moslems, and Buddhists—who devalue life for the sake of the "development of the soul," tend to value their own souls, not the souls of others. And when you're worried about your own karma, there is little time to express much concern for anyone else's.

But God values all people the same, regardless of their beliefs. The result: Christians are supposed to value people because they are people, not for what they believe, do, or are. At least that's the way Christ values them. Unconditionally.

Most of us who follow Jesus are still working on that one. If you believed for certain that people of other religions were going to hell, would you do anything differently than you are currently doing? Probably. That means you don't really believe it.

You really believe only that which activates you.

You're Very Expensive

I wrote this chapter that you might come to understand your worth. And those around you have the same worth. A huge price was paid for you. I want you to understand the truth of that statement to the extent that you would devote the rest of your days to keeping souls out of hell. Part of the difficulty is that most people don't understand the value of their souls.

Low self-image problems are pandemic. Most of us have a poor one. People with good ones usually have them for the wrong reasons. That's one of the causes of mid-life crisis. It's a time of life when we find we're not such hot stuff after all. Or it's a time when we find we've been chasing the wrong dream. The perception of having very little value or greatly diminished value in the middle of your life can be a cruncher.[53]

I attended a Pro Athletes Outreach conference for NFL football players and their wives. Tony Campolo and I were the primary speakers. Norm Evans, president of Pro Athletes Outreach, a former all-pro lineman, and wearer of a beautiful Super Bowl ring (he has another in his drawer at home), was asked by Tony to stand up in front of the group.

"Norm," Tony spit as he screamed, "you were once a sperm."

Everyone fell out laughing in disbelief.

Tony continued, "One day five million of those little guys lined up for a race down a long tube. And Norm, I have great news for you—you won." His point . . . Norm is uniquely special and a winner.

What Jesus did for you, the way He did it, and why makes you valuable beyond your wildest dreams.

Do you have a deeper understanding of the value of a soul? I hope so.

Now couple your understanding of value with the reality that nice people really do go to hell.

If you do, your life will never be the same. How could it be?

Chapter Nine
MAKIN' SENSE?
(Conclusions for the person who believes.)

The most significant day in my ministry occurred during a high-school raft rally on the Deschutes River in Oregon. Over 260 teenagers attacked the rapids, four or five folks in two-man rafts, each with a life jacket and an oar. Can you imagine over sixty rafts strung out in stretches of wilderness? It was wild!

We arrived on a Sunday and set up camp at an old rodeo fairground not far from the river. The plan was to raft on Monday, Wednesday, and Friday. The last day would take us to the Columbia River and we would drive back to Portland. Tuesday and Thursday were play days in camp. I spoke each evening.

Sunday night was chaos. We gathered in the grandstand. A spotlight totally blinded me. Moths danced around the light throwing shadows across my face. I couldn't see beyond the first row. Crowd control was impossible. The kids were noisy. Few wanted to be at the meeting. Everyone was looking forward to the next day. And I was supposed to speak.

People were poking each other, laughing and talking while I was doing my thing. Groups were drifting to the upper recesses of the grandstand where little good occurs. Couples were sneaking off to the bushes. I was speaking.

On Monday we rafted all day. That night exhausted campers were suffering from anticipation-letdown and sunburn. The last place they wanted to be was at a meeting. Most fell asleep while I spoke, which meant they were wired for the rest of the night, after I finished the talk. My amen only woke them up. It was quite a night.

Tuesday was an in-camp play day. One teenage boy came up to me while we were waiting in line and said, "Mr. Carty, I absolutely and totally disagree with everything you have said so far."

"What's your name?

"Dan."

"Dan, do you know Jesus?"

"No sir, I don't."

"Well Dan, no wonder you disagree. Why don't you continue to listen for a couple more days and then let's talk. I don't think we have enough to talk about yet, but join me for lunch anyway."

Then I met Scott. He was five feet, nine inches tall, weighed 265 pounds, and was 4-percent body fat. Scott was a walking manhole cover. He had brought his friend George to camp hoping he would get saved.

Tuesday night I spoke again. I had planned to give the kids an opportunity to receive Christ. At the beginning of the meeting the same things were happening: crawling into the rafters, sneaking into the bushes, and lots of talking. But halfway through the meeting something happened. I had never experienced it before and I have yet to experience it again. I can only describe it as the Holy Spirit coming upon the meeting.

Kids started sneaking back into the meeting from the bushes. The folks in the rafters came down and joined the group. It got stone silent. All were in a state of expectation. People packed in tightly. God was going to do something and you didn't have to be a believer to know it.

I finished my message and gave a call to those who wanted to know Him. Fifty-two young people responded. It remains the most powerful night I have ever experienced in ministry. Repentance was rampant. Tears of brokenness flowed. Lives were renewed. But neither Dan nor George were among the horde of new believers.

We left the grandstand to go to a room under the bleachers to counsel the group. On the way my eyes met Dan's. He turned on a dime and ran down a row of tents away from me. As it turned out, he went into the wrong tent and a girl led him to the Lord. Dan couldn't run away from God any longer. I didn't see George.

The next day I was in the boat with Scott and George. Scott was frustrated. He believed with all his heart that his friend George was headed for hell and he was determined to do all he could about being a part of changing that.

As we were preparing the boat to enter a major rapid, Scott yelled to his friend, "George, you never know when something might happen. A person ought to be ready!" And with those words, Scott threw George out of the boat.

Well, the boat came down the rapid okay. And so did George. When we entered the calm water at the bottom of the rapids we paddled over and Scott reached out to George, one-handed him up, over, and into the boat and without smiling, said, "See what I mean?"

We laughed; George and Scott didn't. Their eyes were saying things to the other, but their lips did not move. I couldn't tell what either of them was thinking. Were they mad, hurt, scared, confused, frustrated? It didn't show.

That night, with so many new believers, it was determined that a communion service would be great. We hadn't planned for one and didn't have any elements. But the cook had a big box of Kix cereal, and I knew the snack truck had a few six-packs of Welch's grape soda. They would have to do. God knew our hearts.

So there we were, under the stars, sitting in the grandstands of an old rodeo fairground remembering the body and the blood our Lord so willingly gave for us. It was around 10:30 P.M. when we finished.

After thirty minutes of hugs and saying good night, everyone left the grandstand. Everyone but Scott and George, that is.

They stood and came down to the front row, so I sat down with them. Scott said his friend wanted to know Jesus Christ and be free of his sin. I told him he'd come to the right place.

After praying, Scott asked, "Is it too late to have communion? It will be George's first and it would be great if you would join us."

I scrounged a few leftover Kix and found a can of pop with a few drops left in the bottom. So there we were, sitting in the grandstands under the stars, remembering what Christ did for us—just like we had done for the other new believers. It was around 11:30 P.M. when we finished. George was in the kingdom. And Scott smiled. His passion for the soul of his friend had been rewarded.

Consider the following exhortation:

> The Bible does not give the physical location of hell or anything about its furnishings, but it

> assures readers that those whose sins are not atoned for by Jesus Christ will receive perfect justice from God, that they will receive exactly what they deserve for all eternity, which will be a most miserable fate. This ought to be one of the impelling motives making evangelism the urgent business of all Christians.[54]

This truth sure motivated Scott. It made him a great friend to George and will make him a great neighbor for anyone living next door to him. Scott is a man who won't let your spiritual house burn down without a fight. Why?

Depth of belief regulates commitment.

Since he fully believes in the value of a soul and that nice people go to hell, he'll do anything in his power to make sure those God puts in his path encounter Christ.

I Wanna' Be Like Scott

I have three motives for writing this book: 1) to convince you that nice people really do go to hell; 2) to play a part in solving your problem if you are a nice person going there; and 3) to demonstrate the value of a soul. My hope is that the three concepts will combine in your mind to change your life to become like Scott. He is an example of how I want to be, and what I'd like you to become. Scott loved his friend so much he risked their relationship to show him the truth.

Also notice that Scott had so developed his friendship with George that he had earned the right to be straightforward with him—even to the point of throwing him out of the boat. Be careful about walking up to folks and dumping the whole gospel load on them right away. Ask God if that's what He wants you to do before you do it. Some people are called by God to do that, but most of us should develop relationships with people to the point where we have earned the right to throw them in the river. But either way, understand the risks. Those who refuse to hear will probably turn on you. You'll be ridiculed and put down. The result—you'll be persecuted for your faith.

Persecution Along the Way

J. Vernon McGee said that the Christian life isn't easy . . . it's impossible. One thing is certain: There will be trials along the way, especially for those who understand the value of a soul. People picked on Scott. Not physically. You don't do that with someone who is 265 pounds and 4-percent body fat. But they bad-mouthed him—teased him about his faith. He made other Christians uncomfortable because of his zeal. Persecution seems to come to those who take a stand for Christ.

It sure wasn't easy for Richard Wurmbrandt. He got persecuted big-time.

In his classic book *Tortured for Christ,*[55] the great Romanian pastor recounts his experiences at the hands of the Communists during their rule of his country. I've paraphrased his story for the sake of time and space.

They told him not to preach. He preached. They warned him again. But he preached. So Wurmbrandt was thrown into prison.

But this wasn't your ordinary cell. It wasn't high enough to stand up in and wasn't long enough for him to stretch out. In addition, his cruel captors tortured the pastor every other day. Every day would have killed him, so they did it every other day. For eight years. There is no part of Wurmbrandt's body that does not have multiple scars.

Richard Wurmbrandt thought he was in hell itself. Only the daily ration of moldy bread and stale water brought reality into the situation. And all he had to do to be set free was promise not to preach.

My late friend Dave Sundquist told me about the time Wurmbrandt was in the pulpit of a large church in Florida. A huge choir had just sung a particularly beautiful song. As Wurmbrandt began, he spoke of the beauty of the music. "That was lovely," he said, "but it's not the most beautiful music I have ever heard. Actually, the most beautiful music I ever experienced came out of the cells of men and women who were being persecuted for their faith. There is a song we would sing for hours, sometimes even all night long. I don't have a very good voice but I'll try to sing it for you."

As he backed away from the microphone, Wurmbrandt stunned the audience by screaming at the top of his lungs three times.

AHHHHHHHHHH! UGGGGHHHHHHHH! OOOOOHHHHHHHHHH!

The shrieks pierced the silence and shocked all who heard. The congregation sat paralyzed and dazed.

Wurmbrandt continued, "That's the most beautiful music I have ever heard. Men and women lying in a pool of their own blood, screaming from the pain of torture, sometimes all night long. And they did so because they refused to compromise their faith."

The Bible makes it clear. Those who would take a stand for their faith will be blessed, but they will also be persecuted. The Christian walk is not an easy trip.

You probably will not have to endure the kind of persecution Richard Wurmbrandt had to face. Unless you end up in a third-world country as a missionary or get kidnapped and sacrificed by satanists, it's not likely ever to be a concern of yours.

At this writing, my daughter is preparing to go overseas with Wycliffe Bible Translators. When she made the announcement I experienced the same emotions the first time my son beat me in basketball. It was bittersweet.

In previous years I had never let him beat me when we played ball together. Oh, I did keep our games close. After all, I didn't want him to lose interest. But I never let him beat me. When that happened I wanted it to be a really big deal. The greatest day in his basketball career, to that point, was beating me one-on-one. That's what he told the press secretary at the university when he entered.

After our game I was thrilled for him. But I was sad for me. Age had taken its toll. I was excited to pass my baton on to my son. He would have to be a much better player than me to be competitive at the college level, so I was excited for him. It was happening and a college scholarship would save me $75,000. But the old man was rapidly becoming a spectator, and that was hard. That's what I meant by bittersweet.

Having your daughter embrace your faith to the point that it becomes her own, to the degree that she wants to spend her life serving the God you love, is the thrill of a lifetime. There is nothing like it. But at the same time, when she wants to do it in some third-world environment, well now, that's something else altogether. Kim's going to get parasites for Jesus and malaria for God. The grandkids will be so far away, and they'll probably get malaria, too. I can't protect her over there. She has a husband who does that now, anyway. I'll really have to give her to God—in reality, not just with words.

I'm happy, sad, excited, and terrified. Happy because she's sold out to Jesus. Sad because the apron strings will be severed. Excited because God's giftedness in her is being fulfilled. Terrified because what happened to Richard Wurmbrandt could happen to her. Mine is truly a bittersweet reaction.

What happened to Wurmbrandt, and what could happen to Kim, is not likely to happen to you or me. But it could be that the Romanian pastor had it easier than you or me. Perhaps what he went through wasn't as difficult as what we have to face. You see, Richard Wurmbrandt faced the full fury of the devil in a frontal assault. He was not confronted with subtle temptation. His was an all-or-nothing decision. The issue wasn't compromise; it was total resignation. Stand or fall. Persevere or cave in.

Make no mistake. Wurmbrandt's salvation was not in jeopardy. He was secure in Christ and no external torment could separate him from God, regardless of any words they might have forced him to say. The issue was the building up or tearing down of the man's faith. Belief was being put to the test. He was being fitted for service in God's crucible for big responsibilities. Wurmbrandt was not confronted with subtle, erosive decisions. This was an all-or-nothing encounter.

Let me ask a hard question. Do you think it was easier for him to endure his trial than it is for you to get through the temptations in your world? Having never been in an all-or-nothing situation, I don't know for sure, but it might be easier to stand firm in the face of full-on attack than to consistently keep from falling to subtle compromise.

That is what you have to face—subtle compromise. A little cave-in here, a little cave-in there, and after four or five compromises your faith is left in the same shambles as if you had folded all at once.

> *The compromise that erodes a person's faith more thoroughly than any other is the failure to tell your nice friends who are going to hell about Jesus Christ.*

That's one way the devil will probably try to defeat you. A failure to share here. A missed opportunity there. Catching you at times of weakness or fatigue. Knowing you should, but not having the courage, and then having to live with the lame excuses you came up with. It's terribly defeating.

Or, having your friend turn on you and put you down hard when you are trying to help can keep you down, too. It's a faith cruncher. When you love enough to risk the relationship and then see the association go up in smoke, it's tough. It takes a lot of faith to overcome fear and endure persecution.

The Faith/Commitment Proportion

Wurmbrandt endured because of the depth of his faith. He firmly believed that preaching the gospel was more important than his life. He believed nice people really do go to hell. As a matter of fact, he so thoroughly believed it, he chose to endure torture in prison rather than live without being able to tell people how to avoid eternal judgment.

You can tell about the depth of Richard Wurmbrandt's belief by the depth of his commitment. Wurmbrandt believed to the max. That is the only way he could have endured to the max.

Nice people really do go to hell. What you are going to do about it depends on the degree to which you believe it. Commitment problems are nothing more than belief problems. A tiny commitment means a puny belief.

I hope you believe that nice people really do go to hell. If you do, you'll do something about it. If you don't, you won't.

> *How you spend your time, talent, and treasure over the course of your life will measure the depth and breadth of your commitment and belief.*

When Concepts Collide

I contend that when a person fully believes nice people go to hell and knows there is nothing more valuable than a soul, the person will never be the same. When those two concepts collide, a passion for the souls of people will result and the person's ambition and the use of his resources will be focused on diminishing the population of the pit.[56] If that doesn't happen, then the person must not believe.

Remember what Jesus told us in Matthew 7:13-14. Most people will end up choosing hell over heaven. So don't think of it as a numbers game. The task appears overwhelming. But anyone can eat an elephant if he'll keep at it. Concentrate on the worth of an individual soul. That will keep you going. Tell people what Jesus has done for you and what He has done for them. Most folks will reject what you have to say, but a few will decide to follow Him. Remember the ninety-nine sheep? It will be worth whatever you have to go through to save one.

Be prepared for "Christians" to be the cause of your greatest grief. They'll sap and steal your energy if you let them. Your zeal will make them uncomfortable, and they'll end up putting you down. You may even get lonely. Those who have a passion for the things of God frequently have to walk alone. The following story tells how it might be for you.

An earthen retaining dam had just burst. There had been plenty of notice. Everyone downstream had been warned. All were safe. But the water had rushed out so fast that fish had been left flipping and flopping, dying in the mud. A boy was running about throwing as many as he could into the stream which the lake had become.

Rather than helping, a man who had been watching hollered at the boy, "Hey sonny, don't work so hard. You can't save them all. There are too many for you. What you're doing isn't going to matter much."

The boy had a fish in his hand when he heard the man; he gave it a heave, and with a splash the fish darted out of sight into the depths of the stream. "Tell him that," the boy yelled with a smile of satisfaction, pointing to the ripples on the water. Without looking back, he kept on working but concluded, "At least I'm doing what I can." Wishing he could do more, the boy had to be content doing what he could. But he didn't let the man slow him down.

What a shame to be like the man. Sitting, doing nothing, and trying to make those who are doing something feel bad about doing it.

Be like the boy. Don't just sit there criticizing those who are doing something. The next time you see a street-corner evangelist, encourage him. It may not be your thing, but don't be threatened by what he's doing. When you see John 3:16 written on a poster in the background on TV during some sporting event, remember, it's someone doing what he can. It may not be your bag, but don't put him down. The dancer who uses her aerobics class to conduct a weekly Bible study, the man who uses Toastmasters to develop his testimony, the folks who are helping at the rescue mission—encourage them. They're doing what they can. I think Campus Crusade's quote is a good one: "The evangelism I'm doing is better than the evangelism you're not doing."

What can you do that few others can do? What do you like to do? How can you develop a ministry around it? Do what you can in spite of those who don't understand, because nice people really do go to hell.

In this chapter I spoke primarily to believers. If you now have a fresh understanding and excitement about the value of a soul and the eternal danger facing so many, you will probably want to do something about it.

You may be the next Ruth or Billy Graham. I don't know. But it's not likely. It's okay to think big, just start small. Bloom where you're planted and let God validate your ministry. You may be called to save the world, but your calling will more likely be to save your corner of it.

You don't have to try to fit into someone else's mold unless it is right for you. You can be creative. Don't be afraid to fashion your ministry around what you like to do.[57]

Have fun going for it. Being a part of God's plan for changing lives is the most rewarding thing I've ever done. I think you'll find it to be true for you, too!

But perhaps you haven't yet received Christ. If that's true, you might still be struggling with this born-again business.

Don't get frustrated. Remain open to what God wants to say to you. And don't give up reading just yet. There is something yet for you to learn. But it's the last button on Jeb's shirt.

Chapter Ten
THE LAST BUTTON ON JEB'S SHIRT
(Conclusions for the person who doesn't believe.)

I was to speak at a men's retreat and had entered the camp dining room for dinner. I joined four guys at their table, made the introductions, and began to eat. The man across from me said, "I have cancer."

That was it. No other words. No lead-in, no preparation, no nothin.' As it turned out, he was telling the truth. He did have cancer. His approach was certainly abrupt, and I didn't know if he was trying to shock me, or if he really wanted a response. I think my reply would have been the same regardless of his motive.

I looked him in the eye and asked, "Are you ready to die?"

He wasn't. He didn't know Christ.

Are you ready to die? You're not if you're lost.

Can you imagine being lost and not knowing it? It happened to my friend Maurice Russell.

Maurice, his son Jeff, and Jeff's dog Uggi went backpacking in the White Mountains of Arizona a few years ago. The goal was to spend a weekend drawing closer to his fifteen-year-old son.

They weren't experienced but they had some equipment, including a tent, sleeping bags, a compass, a map, and a three-day supply of food. Figuring a canteen of water to get them from the trail head to Tonto Creek, they started out eagerly on a sunny Friday morning. It took four hours longer to find water than was planned. After a good drink, a little fishing, and a romp in the creek, the day was over. They enjoyed their first night under the stars and looked forward to two days of hiking up Tonto Creek to Bear Flat.

The hike on Saturday and Sunday was more difficult than either had expected. Actually, it was treacherous. The danger made it much slower going than either of them had prepared for. Jeff had a date on Sunday night and keeping it was real important to him. If they made Bear Flat by noon on Sunday, everything would be fine.

Saturday was a great, but trying, day. They finished it with trout and popcorn. Things were going well. But on Sunday, noon came and went and Bear Flat hadn't come into view. Jeff blamed the whole thing on his dad, and as irritation mixed with disappointment, strong words started flying. So much for bonding. Then it started to rain. Bear Flat was nowhere to be found.

By evening everything was wet, including their sleeping bags, and the food was gone. They had to settle for the uncooked trout they caught. It was too wet to get a fire started.

Jeff had missed saying goodbye to the girl who was going back to her home in the Midwest. He spent the night hot with anger as he shivered in a wet sleeping bag.

The dog was as tired of trout as Maurice and Jeff were, and the walk wasn't fun anymore. Cuts, blisters, scrapes, and irritation filled their thoughts. More words about poor planning and dumb ideas filled the air. They continued to hike, thinking that Bear Flat was around the next bend in the creek—but it never was.

The compass looked like the rain had ruined it. It indicated they were going northeast, yet they knew they were going north. And north was where they would find Bear Flat. Besides, they had to stay with the creek. At least it provided water and food, and they knew it flowed into the flat. They didn't bother with the compass anymore; it was unreliable. And they knew Maurice's wife Nancy would be worried. She didn't know they were fine. It was simply further to Bear Flats than they thought and the trip required more time than they had set aside.

On Tuesday, being over twenty-four hours overdue, they saw a plane in the sky that they thought might be looking for them. Jeff had spotted a helicopter on the horizon, too. So they spread out a white sheet and flashed a signaling mirror. They were too tired and hungry to travel right away anyhow.

Forty-five minutes later, as they were breaking camp, a hello came from behind them. It was a National Guardsman. The helicopter had dropped him off and gone back for fuel. After a half-hour hike to a clearing, the helicopter appeared. Five minutes later they were at the coordination headquarters where a crew had been directing over fifty people in the search.

Never once had either Maurice or Jeff thought they were lost. They just assumed they hadn't yet arrived. But they had taken a wrong turn and had been walking up Hegler Creek, not Tonto Creek. It was a common mistake. The rescuers knew right where to find them. Father and son had been lost . . . but neither had known it.

There are a lot of nice people out there who have taken the wrong turn in life and are walking up the wrong canyon toward what they think is Bear Flat. *If I lead a good life I'll be just fine*, conclude most. *Nice people don't really go to hell*. They are lost and don't know it.

People choose to believe their own reasoning over trustworthy sources. It happens all the time. Trusting our instincts over a compass isn't uncommon. Neither is trusting the philosophies of men over the directions of God. Why do people continue to rely on themselves and treat the Bible like it's all wet? Because they are lost and don't know it.

Yes, it's possible to be lost and not know it. That was Maurice's problem. It might have been yours, but not anymore. I've been careful to tell you the whole story. Nice people really do go to hell. You may be lost, but at least you know it.

It is one thing to be lost and not know it, but it's quite another to be lost, know it, and not acknowledge it.

My backpacking buddy Don Snow directs the Rocky Mountain High program for Officers' Christian Fellowship out of Spring Canyon in Colorado. They conduct Christ-centered outback experiences for military personnel. He told me a great story that fits right here.

One drizzly evening in July, a pack train had brought a barbecued chicken dinner surprise to the participants. At high altitudes, hypothermia is always a concern, so a soft rain is never to be taken lightly. And dehydration is an ever-present threat. A person has to drink a surprising amount of water to stay hydrated. These are just two mountain killers. Getting struck by lightning, falling into crevasses, and getting lost are other good ways to die.

As dinner was cooking, a family in wet shorts and T-shirts came walking by. Everyone was shivering and thirsty. The dad was macho. Mom and the two teenage boys were miserable and let it show. They had climbed Mt. Yale that day but they had come down the wrong canyon and gotten lost for over five hours. They hadn't had food or water since morning.

"Where's a trail?" were the first words out of the man's mouth. It embarrassed him to have to ask.

Noticing he had said *a* trail, not *the* trail, Don replied, "We'll have some food in about ten minutes and a hot drink in about five. Looks like you folks could use some refreshment."

The woman and the boys were nodding and looking relieved when the dad shattered their hopes. "Nah, we don't need nothin.' Just tell me where a trail is."

"Well, it's about fifty meters right through the woods."

"When I get to the trail which way do I go?"

"Where's your car? "

"It's at Denny Creek trail head."

"You go down."

"When I get down and I get to the road, what do I do?"

Don told him to turn and go back up the hill. The man was so lost he didn't even know if he should go up or down when he got to the main road.

As soon as they left Don told his people, "That was a really good example of how folks die in the woods. They were lost and confused, cold and hungry, but he wouldn't say, 'Yeah, we could use some help.' He wouldn't even let the members of his family eat or drink."

Harold, the wrangler who brought the food for the barbecue, is a fun cowboy. He was reflecting on the coming and going of the family. "My truck was down there," he said. "I could have driven them to their car. It's gonna' be plum dark before they get where they're a goin.'"

We wondered why the man wouldn't accept the help he needed. Our conclusion? Pride! He put himself and the members of his family in jeopardy because of his pride. Mr. Macho didn't want his family to receive help because he refused to admit it was his lostness that had gotten them in trouble.

The actions of Don and Harold remind me of a story Ron Carlson told at Hume Lake during the summer of '91. I don't know it word for word but what follows is close.

A man who didn't know how to swim fell in the water. Mohammed, Buddha, and Jesus Christ were on the shore.

"Please help me!" shouted the drowning man.

Mohammed said, "I must not interfere with your development." He stood there passively.

Buddha began yelling instructions on how to to swim but stayed on the shore.

Jesus Christ jumped in, took the man to safety, calmed him down, and then stood in shallow water and taught him how to swim.

My friend Don Snow tried to be like Christ to that vain, shivering father. He offered food and drink to meet the family's immediate need. He was ready to guide them down the canyon to make sure they were safe. And Harold had a truck for them to drive to where they were parked. Everything the family needed was available to them. But the dad was too proud.

Are you a parent who is lost? Which way are you leading your children? Acknowledge your lostness and change directions, for their sake as well as yours!

Are you a teenager who has been going the wrong way? Are your friends doing the same? Confess it. Change destinations.

There's a strong word that describes those who are too proud to receive help when they need it. The man in the mountains filled all the criteria: fool. So does anyone who denies the probabilities of hell. It's so hard to convince some people. Facts don't mean much to a fool. I guess that's why the Bible has so much to say about him.

"The way of a fool seems right to him, but a wise man listens to advice" (Proverbs 12:15). The sixty-six books of the Bible, written by forty authors, over a period of sixteen hundred years, in several countries, in three languages, being in perfect harmony with each other and all other historical, archaeological, and scientific works is a miracle of God's preservation that can't be denied. Only a fool would fail to heed its advice.

"The discerning heart seeks knowledge, but the mouth of a fool feeds on folly" (Proverbs 15:14). To deny the reality of hell when the Bible speaks about it more than any other topic is foolish indeed.

"A fool finds no pleasure in understanding but delights in airing his own opinions" (Proverbs 18:2). God has made Himself crystal clear. Of what use is man's opinion when it contradicts God? Only a fool would listen to a fool, and only a fool would speak against the Father.

"As a dog returns to its vomit, so a fool repeats his folly" (Proverbs 26:11). Some people never learn. Only a fool continues to stand in opposition to God.

I was exposed to fools some years ago when I was at UCLA working toward a doctorate in public health. I have often thought back to a research project in which I was involved.

A group was given a series of driver-reaction tests. The time it took each person to move his right foot from the gas pedal to the brake pedal in response to a visual stimulus was measured. Then the subjects each consumed two beers and sat for ten minutes. Afterward, the reaction test was administered again. Although alcohol levels were well below the definition of legal intoxication, the reaction times of every test subject were significantly slower.

That part of the study was not surprising. But in each instance, those being tested felt their reaction times after drinking the two beers was better than before. They were all surprised by the findings. Further, it was very difficult to convince them that the data was correct because it so completely went against what they thought was true. Several even chose to reject the findings in favor of their own perceptions, and still feel the same way today.

The study reminds me of the old saying, "I've made up my mind. Don't confuse me with the facts." It's the response of a fool.

Dear friend, consider this carefully. If the Bible is God's Word, then it must contain the facts. It has clearly established itself to be God's revelation to us and it emphatically says that nice people really do go to hell. You may not think those statements are true, and you may be sincere in your belief. But which is more likely to be correct—you or the Bible? "Me!" is the response of a fool.

Are you one of those who have had a couple of beers? You think you're just fine, don't you? *How could a loving God send somebody like me to hell?* Is that your thought? *There will be a whole lot of genuinely bad people going before I do.* Is that your conclusion? Your mixed-up perception of God has given you an inflated opinion of yourself. You're an onion who is acting just like a bunch of Philistines I read about.

Dagon Dummies

Sometimes the facts don't change a thing. In 1 Samuel 5:1-12 the Philistines had captured the ark of God (the box Indiana Jones went looking for in *Raiders of the Lost Ark*). They took it into the temple of their god Dagon and set the ark beside the idol. The next day Dagon was found face down before the ark of the Lord.

Phil, the Philistine leader, had the idol returned to its place, but the next morning Dagon was down again. This time his head and hands had been broken off.

Then God brought a heavy hand on the area around the Philistine temple in the form of devastation, affliction of young and old, panic, tumors, and death. It got so bad the people wanted God's box outta there. So they gave it back to Israel.

After those events the Philistine folks knew the God of the ark of the Jews had authority over Dagon. And they clearly acknowledged the heavy hand of God upon them. This God of the Jews was supreme and the people of the land knew it. Word travels fast. "There is no God like the God of the Bible," is basically what they said. You know that too, don't you?

The Philistines got rid of the ark when God sent tumors and death upon them. They knew the source of their troubles. God had gotten their attention. But did the dummies transfer their worship? No way! They stuck with Dagon. Why? Pride!

Pride's a Problem

Is pride your problem? Is it your Dagon? Give it up. It can't stand up to God. Don't be like the Philistines, who stuck with their god. Don't be like that backpacking husband—a prideful, arrogant know-it-all who didn't know a thing, who put his loved ones at risk because of his unwillingness to seek help. Don't be like the fools who refuse to admit they care more about drinking than the welfare of those driving on the highways with them.

Are you aware of your lostness but have yet to do anything about it? I'm sure you're a nice person, but if you don't know Jesus Christ as your Savior, you have a huge problem. You are going to hell. Do something! But make it the right something. Any ol' something won't solve your problem.

The Last Button on Jeb's Shirt

My dad has some great old Missouri sayings. One of them is, "We're down to the last button on Jeb's shirt." It means we're almost through.

I've said it as many ways as I can. I've driven my editor nuts by using more illustrations than I'm supposed to. I've been redundant beyond words. I've broken all the rules of writing. But I'd rather mess up by saying it too many times in too many ways than fail to say it enough. Now we really are down to the last button on Jeb's shirt.

Do you believe me yet? Do you believe that nice people really do go to hell?

You now know that if the whole deal is real you are lost if you don't know Christ. I assume you believe that. Gallup says that most Americans do. If so, the decision you are now faced with is to acknowledge your lostness. If you refuse to do that, I can't do any more for you. I've taken my best shot.

If you believe nice people go to hell and take ownership of the problem by recognizing yourself as the onion you are, there is still one more step—take a close look at the Son of God. Have an encounter with Him and see what happens. Few there are who have met Jesus Christ who have come away unchanged. Ask Him for help and He will gladly give it. Ask Him into your life and He will come in. If you do, you'll never be the same. Actually, you probably won't be the same even if you don't—but then you won't be saved from your sin.

You'll Never Be the Same

Pilate couldn't wash his hands enough. Although he didn't become a Christian, his meeting with Jesus Christ had permanently changed him. After trying four times to release Jesus, he followed through on ordering His death. But Pilate would never be the same. Christ had left His mark on the man.

So it was with the soldier at the foot of the cross. "Surely this man must be the Son of God," he said. Or maybe he prayed. We're not sure which. Either way, he was a changed man. If he prayed, the Roman was also a saved man. If he gave only intellectual assent, he is still lost in his sin.

We don't know about those who tried to throw Jesus off a cliff. Just before they tried to toss Him, our Lord turned and walked away through their midst. Liken that occurrence to a Jew walking out of Auschwitz in broad daylight, or a black man walking away from a midnight Ku Klux Klan 'gater trolling party. It had to have gotten somebody's attention. Do you think the observers would ever be the same?

My favorite encounter of all was with the cohort of soldiers marching into the Garden of Gethsemane before daylight, the morning Judas betrayed Jesus.

In the Roman army a cohort was at least fifty men. On

one occasion it was six hundred. But usually a cohort represented three hundred soldiers.

However, these soldiers were Jewish temple guards. Matthew called them a large crowd, while Mark and Luke refer to a crowd. Elsewhere in John the translation "detachment" or "detail" is used. So we don't know how many there were marching through the city that morning before daylight to arrest one man.

Imagine—little hob-nailed sandals. You could hear 'em all over town stirring up dust in the stillness of that hour. Townspeople were probably getting up and following.

Little leather miniskirts. Little tassels on their heads. What a sight!

"Halt, one two!" shouted the captain as he approached the man Judas had kissed. "Are you the guy they call Jesus?" he demanded of the Son of God.

"I am he," is how your Bible says Jesus responded. But that's a poor translation. What Christ really said was, "I AM!" Don't be mistaken about what He said. He wasn't merely acknowledging His identity. "I AM" is something else indeed. That's the name that came out of the burning bush that talked to Moses. It was the name of Yahweh, the unspeakable name of God. A Jew would never say it. But Jesus had just screamed what amounted to, "I'm God, and you're lookin' at Him!"

The power of Jesus speaking that name made bowling pins out of the cohort. All the macho soldiers were knocked on their macho behinds. Neither Josephus, nor any contemporary historian ever refuted the occurrence. My friend, it is historical fact.

I can see one of those big, burly dudes standing up, dusting off his rear end, and asking, "Hey, what was that?"

His buddy pointed toward Jesus and replied, "I don't

know, but it came out of His mouth."

And with a huge smile I can imagine Jesus saying, "Okay, you can take Me now. I just wanted you to know who you were messin' with."

Do you think the soldiers would ever forget that day? I doubt it. They might not have entered into a personal relationship with Jesus, but they would never be the same.

That's the way it was in those days when you encountered Jesus. That's the way it is today, too. That's the way it will be for you. Few there are who encounter Jesus who walk away unchanged. You may not receive Jesus Christ, but you will never be the same.

It's Time to Take Temptation Captive

It is time for your encounter with Jesus.

Are you ready?

Stop reading for a moment and think about your answer to the following question.

Who do you say that He is?

You're close aren't you?

I guarantee that satan won't let you get away easily. What you think about next may determine where you'll spend eternity.

There was a very attractive girl, twenty-five, a virgin (the only one she knew), doing her thing for God. She loved the Lord and was active in the singles department in her church.

One day a handsome hunk walked up to her.

"You're incredible," he said to her. "I've never been attracted to anyone like I am to you. Tell you what. Today is Thursday. Tomorrow is the start of a long weekend. You don't have to be back to work until Tuesday. But, if you take a day off and return on Wednesday, we'll have time to go to my villa in Hawaii for the weekend. The food will be great and we'll enjoy each other to the fullest. What do you say?"

The girl was caught totally off guard. The guy of her dreams had just approached her with the prospect of a phenomenal weekend, the likes of which she had never dreamed possible. But before she could respond, he pulled out his checkbook, filled one out for a million dollars, dated it for Wednesday, tore it out, and handed it to her. "That's how badly I want to go to Hawaii with you," he said as his green eyes pierced her loneliness.

Her thoughts went crazy. *I'll never have to work again. I can live off the interest. I'm the only virgin I know. All my friends are doing it. I'll do it just once. I'll confess it on Thursday.*

She thought and pondered. Wouldn't you?

Don't get too uppity and judgmental about her thoughts of confessing it on Thursday. We all play cheap grace games with God. We know He'll forgive us seventy times seven so we try to take advantage of Him. Somehow we think we'll be better off doing what we want to do and obtaining forgiveness later. We think we can sin and not have lasting consequences. So like Magic Johnson we dash off to play in the traffic, thinking we'll return unscarred.

She thought about it and found her hand reaching for the check as she said, "Okay."

He pulled it back and shocked her with his next question. "How about that motel over there for thirty bucks?"

She was indignant. "Why, what do you think I am?"

"We've already determined that, haven't we?" was his convicting and condemning answer. "Now we are just negotiating."

What was the girl's problem? Listen closely. She thought about it!

Eve saw the fruit on the tree, thought about it, and ate. The order of events can be reversed. Lot heard about Las Vegas (Sodom), thought about it, and then when he had the opportunity to go to the left or the right, he chose Las Vegas. But that decision had been made years before by thinking about it so much.

You must take your thoughts captive to the obedience of Christ.[58] Don't allow yourself to think about that tempting thought. Satan doesn't want you to consider Jesus.

Distractions?

I know how the devil works. Your mind is wandering right now. You're having trouble concentrating. The phone's been ringing or someone has come to the door. There have been interruptions and distractions. You're having trouble thinking. Isn't that right?

Stop! Consider what's happening. You're in a spiritual battle. And it's over your soul. At least acknowledge that.

You've been trying to live with a foot in each puddle—one in this world and one in God's. But it can't be done. Don't straddle the fence anymore. Get off!

Fence Sitters Are Uncomfortable

I have a passion for your soul. I haven't been awakened in the night in a cold sweat about it, but I do value your soul sufficiently to stay up late writing and to endure the process of editing so that you might read these words. I have spent many an hour thinking through this book and praying for the concepts that might be used to push you over the fence. Here comes the last nudge.

If you are on the devil's side and want to stay there, there isn't much that can be done for you. But if you are straddling the fence, you are probably uncomfortable. That hurts like crazy, especially if you're a guy. I'd love to push you over to the Lord's side.

Why don't you give up? You may never be closer to accepting what Jesus Christ did for you than right now. Why don't you pick up the phone and give God a call?

Pick Up the Phone

This is how the whole deal works.

As I said, my daughter will be on the mission field by the time you read this. Pause for a moment and holler, "Hello, Kim."

You didn't do it, did you? Here we go again. First it's not choosing your number on the goodness scale, and now it's not yelling when I ask you to. You're impossible. You're an onion.

This time do it, okay? Yell as loudly as you can. Put a little something extra into it. Go for it. "Hello, Kim!"

Did she hear you? No. She is too far away.

What's the best way to talk to her? Sure, the telephone.

Do you want to talk to God? Understand that saying, "Oh my God!" won't cut it. That's a worldly exclamation. If you want to talk to God, you have to know His Son.

If the whole deal is real, to talk to God you have to pick up Christ (the phone), and then His Holy Spirit (the wires or microwaves) does the work to make God's phone ring in heaven. Apart from Christ, prayers are nothing more than talking to the floor or the wall. They don't go anywhere. The only prayers He answers, if you don't know Jesus, are the ones that will lead you to Him. And that's the one I want you to pray right now.

It's Time to Act

I have a portable Macintosh computer that I use to write when I'm on the road. "Scrapbook" is a software program that provides a place where text and pictures can be stored for future use. I rarely use it. But as I was working on this chapter, gathering the verses on the fool, there was a piece of text waiting there in "Scrapbook." I do not know the source. I don't remember ever reading it. I certainly don't recall putting it into my computer. So the author is unknown, but the words are perfect as you are confronted with asking Jesus Christ into your life:

> Remember this as you consider your answer. Man has made himself/herself the center of everything in this world. But God will be at the center of everything in heaven. The decision you made or will make, either for or against Christ, should be measurable by what your life revolves around. If it's not God, you won't like heaven. And you probably won't get to go there.

Do you want to stay on the throne of your life, or do you want Jesus Christ to be there?

Consider 1 Chronicles 28:9 before you respond:

> The LORD searches every heart and understands every motive behind the thoughts. *If you seek him, he will be found by you; but if you forsake him, he will reject you forever* (emphasis added).

Those are your options. Seek Him or be forsaken. Put Him in authority of your life or face His judgment. Turn to God; don't trust yourself. Receive what Christ did.

This prayer will help you:

Dear Lord,

You are an awesome God and You know that I don't fully understand everything that's happening right now. This whole thing is too new to me. But I'm responding to what I know is right. Father, I'm a sinner and I want to turn from my sin to You. I realize now that Jesus Christ died for my sin and I want to claim Him for myself.

Jesus, I receive what You did; I want forgiveness, and I want You to have full control of my life. Thank You for coming into my life as You promised and thank You for saving me from hell. I commit myself to a journey of both learning about and serving You.

Does this prayer express where you are? Can you pray it with your heart, as well as your voice? Do you want God in control of every aspect of your life? Then, by the promise of God's Word, the problem of sin and separation from God has been resolved in your life.

Hurray! You made the right choice. You're a winner. Congratulations.

How Do You Feel?

Some people cry. Some people realize how lost they were and weep tears of joy, gratitude, and relief. Some people get very excited, hear bells, gongs, and buzzers, get goose bumps, and whoop and holler over the awareness of their new, intimate relationship with God.

But most don't feel much different at all. Perhaps they sense an inner peace or cleansing knowing that all is finally well with their soul.

So don't depend on feelings for the assurance of your salvation. If you do, you'll always be wondering, *Am I or am I not?* The Bible says that if you confessed with your mouth, and believed with your heart, you are all set:

> If you confess with your mouth, "Jesus is Lord," and believe in your heart that God raised him from the dead, you will be saved. For it is with your heart that you believe and are justified, and it is with your mouth that you confess and are saved (Romans 10:9-10).

Sin Still Will Be a Problem

Even though you're saved from the consequences of your sin, you will still have some old sinful patterns to break. So you'll still blow it now and then (read Romans 7:15-8:2 again and remember that the apostle Paul struggled, too.).[59]

Your new goal is to let Christ in you lengthen your time between stumblings, and when you do stumble, to shorten the time it takes you to confess it with a repentant heart (*see* 1 John 1:9).[60]

Of course, the best goal is to not sin at all. Remember, temptation is not a sin. So that first thought or feeling isn't sin, but dwelling on it is. So claim 1 Corinthians 10:13:

> No temptation has seized you except what is common to man. And God is faithful; he will not let you be tempted beyond what you can bear. But when you are tempted, he will also provide a way out so that you can stand up under it.

You don't have to sin.

If You Received Christ

Nice going! Welcome to the family of God! I'll have the pleasure of meeting you someday and you can tell me all about yourself. Fun, huh?

If you received what Christ did for you, it becomes important to tell a fellow believer and to begin spending some time learning more about what you've done. Therefore, call the person who gave you this book or the church or bookstore where you got it and tell somebody what's happened. Then find a good church where the Bible is taught and start attending regularly. You need to start the process of discipling, or growing in Christ.

If You Have Not Received Christ

My prayer is that God will not reduce the pull on you nor will He give up on you, but instead will grant you more time. However, please remember:

> The LORD searches every heart and understands every motive behind the thoughts. If you seek him, he will be found by you; but if you forsake him, he will reject you forever (1 Chronicles 28:9).

That was my next-to-last shot. I'm nearing the end of my appeal. I'm running out of things to say. I have reasoned with you as best I know how. When reason fails, however, resort to the facts. It's not a bad idea.

As I've said before, you don't have to get a frontal lobotomy to become a Christian. You can remain a thinking person and believe in Jesus Christ. As a matter of fact, I think those who choose to not look at the facts are the foolish ones. The facts will confirm your faith. They won't erode it.

We've come so far together. Take a few more minutes to consider some good, foundational reasons for a solid faith in Christ. Find out if what you believe stands up to the facts. In the final chapter I'll tell you about a few of my favorite reasons for believing. A couple of them are a bit off the wall. But then, you would expect that of me by now, wouldn't you?

Chapter Eleven
WHY THE WHOLE DEAL IS REAL
(A few facts and interesting ideas.)

Thus far we have concentrated on what happens to nice people if the whole deal is real. It's now time to determine whether or not it is. We need some idea of the odds.

Is there a God?

Do the facts support the Bible as being the Word of God?

How real is the whole Christian deal?

Considering the consequences of being wrong (hell), if we can reasonably establish the probability of the whole deal being real, then only a fool would reject eternal life in favor of an eternity in hell. Only a fool or someone who didn't want to submit to God's authority (same thing).

Let's start with God and see if the facts suggest His existence. Some of this ground has been covered in previous chapters, but let's cover a bit more. Understand that volumes have been written in defense of the Christian faith. In the pages that follow I just want to skim the surface of what makes the most sense to me.

Is God for Real?

Most people in the United States believe God is for real. A recent Gallup poll showed 88 percent of Americans said they have never doubted the existence of God. That's strong evidence of God's general revelation at work. Most people believe in God.

The number of those never doubting the existence of God rose with age going from 84 percent for those between eighteen and twenty-four years old, to 93 percent for those over sixty. Remember my story about cooked onions? God uses the problems of life to draw us to Himself. Young people haven't had many problems and therefore see little reason for turning to God. Older people are closer to the end.

Belief declined with education, going from 94 percent for those with less than a high-school education to 78 percent of college graduates. A secular college is not a good place to develop your faith.[61]

My Favorite Reasons for God Being Real

A person's belief doesn't alter the reality of God. God either is or He isn't. I am convinced that there is ample information to establish His reality. I have some favorite reasons.

The Odds

There is a movement afoot to spend government money to search for extraterrestrial life by building a huge antenna/receiver to see if radio wave messages are coming at us from outer space. The primary promoter of the project is a devout humanist and strongly professing atheist. What's interesting to me is that if he would look the other direction, from his telescope into a microscope, he would find the order he's looking for. He wants to search for sequencing which suggests life, like a Morse code, thereby proving intelligence in space. Here's what he would find if he looked through a microscope.

Amino acids link up to form polypeptides. Polypeptides form proteins. Proteins become the building blocks of the body and get real complex, especially in the form of RNA and DNA.

A specific number of amino acids linked in a precise order are required to form a polypeptide. A mathematician figured the odds of the sequencing happening by chance. Would you believe six hundred octodecillion to one (that's six times ten with fifty-eight zeros stretched after it).[62] My friend, that is *way* beyond all reasonable probability. The fool continues to look for ordered messages from the stars while refusing to see the message in God's ordered creation.

Where did the remarkably small color cameras that see in three dimensions (we call them eyes) come from? Who thought up your thumb? Nothing gets close to the complexity of your brain. Your design is wondrous. Something intelligent is responsible for your being here.

It was God who put order into the universe. There is intelligence behind it all. The odds on that statement not being true are just too remote to take an eternal chance.

The Law of the Sail Squirrel

Order doesn't come from disorder. The law of the sail squirrel verifies it. Technically it's called the Second Law of Thermodynamics.

When you run over a squirrel with your car, the animal doesn't get better. Rather, it gets flatter and flatter and dryer and dryer. Pretty soon you can pick it up by the tail and sail it like a frisbee. Dead squirrels become sail squirrels. They don't recover.

Meat spoils, fruit rots, and I age. Everything that's ever been observed winds down. Nothing in life has ever wound up. And if you take the God of creation out of the start-up formula for creation, you would have to have a wind-up that goes beyond possibility. It requires far more faith to believe creation is an accident than to believe there is a God who made all this happen.

Atheists have more faith than I do. They have to. It takes more. My good friend and spiritual papa Ken Poure has a great formula that represents an atheist's faith. Nothing plus nobody equals everything. It takes more faith than I've got to believe that.

Think of a piano. Where did it come from?

Did it always exist? Give me a big break.

Is it the result of random, catastrophic atmospheric conditions? Perhaps. Let me paint a possible scenario.

In the midst of a terrific storm a tree is knocked down. As it falls it hits some rocks and pieces of the log are knocked off and caught up in a tornado-like funnel. The wood bumps and grinds as it flies through the air, being shaped by the debris carried with it.

While that is happening, volcanic action forces molten metal through various-sized fissures in the ground and the strands are chopped off by another falling tree (squuuirt-chommmp). These wires are caught up in the air with the wood.

About that time some little spinners come from somewhere (I don't have that figured out yet) and implant themselves into the wood (buzzzzzzet). That's when some wood stain comes flying by (splaaaaaaat) which is followed by some steel wool (ruuuuuuuuub). It is then that an elephant walks by and loses his tusks in the force of the wind (yaaaaaaaank) and the ivories get tickled as the keys are fashioned, formed, and laid down.

As the cataclysm continues, lightning flashes and thunder roars. After a while we have deposited on the ground . . . taaaaa dummmmm . . . a piano!

What do you think?

What's interesting is that I can't prove it didn't happen that way. But let me give you an option that's infinitely more probable.

I have never seen him, touched him, or smelled him. I wouldn't recognize him if I saw him on the street. But my guess is that there is a piano maker. Why? Because there is a piano and it's a whole lot easier to believe that somebody made it than to believe it happened by chance.

Do you really believe some lightning hit some ooze and made yooz? No way! There must be a people maker. His name is God.

More Time Means Less Probability

Some scientists believe that more time gives random chance more opportunity to occur. But that's just not true. Consider the following illustration.

Take twenty-six, three-foot-by-three-foot pieces of cardboard and put one letter on each card, spell out *Nice People Really Do Go to Hell*. Put them in an airplane, fly one thousand feet above your town, and drop them. What are the chances that they will all fall in order, lined up on Main Street, spelling out the name of this book?

"Not so good," you say. Wait a second. The person who says there is no God says that if you give the cards more time they are more likely to fall in an orderly fashion. Let's test that theory.

This time let's fly the plane over your town at fifteen thousand feet. How does that affect our probabilities? My friend, it makes it even more impossible. Winds, currents, breezes, gusts, canyons—all the variables have more time to cause disarray. Time compounds disorder, it doesn't organize it.

The Absence of Transitional Forms in the Fossil Records

The problem with the evolutionary model is that it tends to remove God from the picture. Strictly speaking, if evolution is true, there is no need for God. There are evolutionists who still believe in God, but there are few atheists who aren't evolutionists. Transitional forms are crucial to the correctness of the evolutionary model.

If we happened by chance, there should be many links in the fossil record. But not only is the link between man and ape missing, links are also missing between other life forms. The fossil record is extensive and guess what? Birds are supposed to have evolved from snakes, but although there are lizards that fly, there are no snakes with feathers in the fossils. A lizard that flies is still a lizard, not a transitional form. There just aren't enough good, solid fossils that support evolution. Too many leaps of faith have to be made because there aren't enough transitional forms.

The odds on the correctness of the evolutionary model are affected by the number of transitional forms. The more there are, the more likely evolution is true. Fewer transitional forms means the odds on evolution being right are long indeed. My friend, the fossil record contains a dearth, not a plethora (great words), of transitional forms. The odds suggest creation, not the godless evolutionary model we've been taught.

The Wonder of the Wandering

Let me give you one more contemporary evidence of God's existence before we move on. During Operation Desert Storm against Iraq we had to keep a few hundred thousand troops and support personnel supplied in a part of the world that is hostile to masses of people. We kept soldiers there for over four months, and at one time we had around 550,000 folks to feed, clothe, and keep hydrated. It wasn't an easy task. The situation tested our supply system to the max.

Dr. David Jeremiah, pastor of Scott Memorial Church in the San Diego area, gives some statistics from a retired army general who attends his church.[63] This man took formulas from army supply manuals and applied them to the needs of the Jews who spent some serious time in the same area our troops did, only during Old Testament times.

By the way, few serious anthropologists or archaeologists will argue that three-and-a-half million people spent forty years wandering in an area that was incapable of supporting them. That they did wander there is fact.

The following are the modern calculations from army standards as to what would have been necessary to take care of the Israelites in the wilderness.

Fifteen hundred tons of food would be required each day just to avoid starvation. If they ate like modern Americans, it would have been more like four thousand tons per day. This estimate was written several years ago so the cost is a bit low, but even at the old price tag it would still take five million dollars a day for groceries. They couldn't grow any grain (they wandered), nor could they have possibly maintained large herds. What would the animals eat and where would they drink?

To deliver that much food would require two freight trains, each a mile long, with every car full of supplies.

Can you imagine a line of box cars two miles long arriving every day for forty years? That's a lot of grub.

Where did all that food come from? Give me a plausible answer that doesn't require a miracle. You can't. The answer has to be God! There is no other option. He gave His people a daily dose of two miles of box cars worth of manna every morning. I'm impressed!

How about water? To drink enough liquid to stay alive and to wash a few dishes would have required eleven million gallons of water per day. That's a freight train eighteen hundred cars long making a run every day.

Where did their water really come from? They wandered in the desert. There were no lakes and they were only occasionally near the Jordan River. They couldn't drink salt water from the ocean. The answer again is—God! He used Moses to talk water out of rocks. Wow!

What would it be like to try and camp three-and-a-half million people as they moved from place to place? The army general calculated that it would take 750 square miles (twenty miles wide, thirty-five miles long). That's a section of ground one third the size of Rhode Island. The wanderers would have to find a place that size every time they stopped moving.

God took care of the starting and stopping with a couple of pillars: It was a cloud by day and a fire by night. When it moved, they moved. When it stopped they stopped. Piece of cake!

How about clothes? Remember, there were no catalog stores. You couldn't even find a mall. And there weren't any toll-free 800 numbers either. They didn't grow cotton. It was impossible to keep enough sheep. There was no cloth or thread to speak of. What did they do? How did they clothe themselves?

They didn't. God did. Here's what He said, "During the forty years that I led you through the desert, your clothes did not wear out, nor did the sandals on your feet" (Deuteronomy 29:5). They never had to replace their duds. God never let their mentionables or their unmentionables wear out. That's wild!

For those who have trouble with the reality of miracles, is there any other answer as to how all those folks got supplied with food, water, clothing, and campsites that is better than by God? Nope! That's the only reasonable reply.

Yep! There is a God. And those are my four favorite reasons fer knowin' He's there. Given more time we could talk about my changed life, circumstances where He has intervened on my behalf, power encounters in prayer, and a whole bunch of other events that serve as additional evidence. But then, I am already convinced.

God is definitely not dead. My friend, He's not even sick. He's as real as real can be. Bettin' against His existence is longest of all long shots.

God says He provided a Book of books to tell us everything about what He wanted us to know. So let's look at the Book to see whether or not it is as real a deal as God is.

Is the Bible for Real?

There are as many as forty ancient books claiming to be a superior revelation. All of the others merely talk about God. In the Bible, God talks.

The first book in the Old Testament is Genesis and in the first chapter you'll find the phrase "God said" nine times. The statement "thus says the Lord" appears twenty-three times in the last Old Testament book (Malachi). In between, the phrase "the Lord spoke" appears 560 times in the first five books alone. Isaiah claims that his message came from the Lord over forty times, Ezekiel sixty times, and Jeremiah a hundred times. "The Lord spoke" or "the Lord says" appears more times than I care to count. Pratney says the words "the Lord spoke" or similar phrases occur 3,800 times.[64] The actual number is 3,808.[65]

MacArthur says,

> There are three hundred and twenty direct quotes from the Old Testament in the New Testament. Jesus Christ added His validation as well, by quoting from twenty-four Old Testament books. Consider the impact of Christ's endorsement:
>
> When examining the testimony of Jesus about the Scriptures, we have to accept one of three possibilities. The first is that there are no errors in the Old Testament, just as Jesus taught. Second, there are errors, but Jesus didn't know about them. Third, there are errors and Jesus knew about them, but He covered them up.
>
> If the second is true—that the Old Testament contains errors of which Jesus was unaware—then it follows that Jesus was a fallible man, He obviously wasn't God and we can dismiss the whole thing. If the third alternative is true—that Jesus knew about the errors but covered them up—then He wasn't honest, He wasn't holy, He certainly wasn't God, and again, the entire structure of Christianity washes away like a sand castle at high tide.
>
> I accept the first proposition—that Jesus viewed the Old Testament as the Word of God, authoritative and without error.[66]

New Testament writers refer to the Old Testament some one thousand times in all. "There can be little doubt that the New Testament writers believed that the Old Testament was God's revelation—His inspired Word."[67] But they also knew that what they were writing was God's revelation as well, making the New Testament just as valid as the Old.

There was a four-hundred-year silence between the last book of the Old Testament and the coming of the first New Testament prophet, John the Baptist. Jesus said that John was greater than any of the Old Testament prophets. Then He went on and said that the New Testament prophets would do even greater works than John. Jesus Christ personally validated the words of those who qualified as New Testament writers.

The New Testament authors knew they were writing God's Word, too. They said so. Luke, Peter, Paul, and John all validated their words as being from God, and went on to add their stamp of approval on what the others had written. It is clear, from the first book to the last, God spoke enough times to validate the Bible as being His Word. And Jesus Christ confirmed it as well.

My Favorite Reasons for the Bible Being Real

One author made an interesting proposal to illustrate how miraculous the authorship of the Bible really is:

> If you selected ten people living at the same time in history, living in the same basic geographical area, with the same basic educational background, speaking the same language, and you asked them to write independently on their conception of God, the result would be anything but a united testimony.
>
> It would not help if you asked them to write about man, woman or human suffering, for it is

> the nature of human beings to differ on controversial subjects. However, the biblical writers not only agree on these subjects but on dozens more. They have complete unity and harmony. There is only one story in the Scriptures from beginning to end, although God used different human authors to record it. The supernatural character of the Bible is one reason we believe Christianity to be true.[68]

Imagine pulling together sixty-six published works from forty different authors—the writings of two kings, two priests, a physician, two fishermen, two shepherds, a legalistic theologian, a statesman, a tax collector, a soldier, a scribe, a butler, and twenty-five others from equally diversified backgrounds. What would you have? Agreement? Hardly! You'd have hodgepodge!

Add also that the documents are to be written in three different languages. Will that make the writings more likely to be in harmony? No way! That makes it a lot tougher.

How about the authors having to write on three different continents and from several different countries? You say, "Jay, you're making this impossible." You're right. But let's send the probabilities off the chart.

What if you spread the writings out over sixteen hundred years? Does that add to the confusion? Sure! It's just like taking the plane with the letters spelling *Nice People Really Do Go to Hell* from one thousand feet to fifteen thousand feet and dropping them. Spreading the writing over that much time would make agreement among the writers a miracle. Exactly! Since miracles come from God, we know that's where the Bible came from. The odds on the Bible not being the handiwork of

God are pretty remote. Wouldn't you agree? But there is more evidence in favor of its miraculous nature.

If the Bible really came from God, since He is all-knowing, shouldn't it be accurate scientifically, historically and archaeologically? If God wrote it, shouldn't it pass the triple test?

Of the forty ancient books of "superior revelation," there is only one that stands the triple test of trustworthiness: the Bible.

The Scientific Test

Can you imagine any work of antiquity not contradicting science? Me neither. There are few books more than five years old that have anything to say about science that don't do that.

While the Koran said the world was flat and held up by three elephants and a turtle, God called it a sphere (*see* Isaiah 40:21-22) and said it hung in nothingness (*see* Job 26:7).

It wasn't until the sixteenth century before science discovered the workings of our circulatory system. The Bible said all along that the life of the flesh is in the blood (*see* Genesis 9:4).

The hydrological cycle was put forth by Isaiah. "As the rain and the snow come down from heaven, and do not return to it without watering the earth and making it bud and flourish, so that it yields seed for the sower and bread for the eater" (55:10).

The principle of land mass being balanced by water mass (isostasy) was spoken of by Isaiah as well (*see* 40:12).

It's hard to believe a book written so long ago doesn't contradict current scientific discovery. What are the odds on that happening? John MacArthur noted, "God wrote the Bible for men of all ages and while His Word never contradicts science, it also never gets trapped into describing some precise scientific theory that becomes outdated in a few years, decades or centuries."[69] Josh McDowell observed the same thing but reported it with a twist: "Where the Bible speaks on matters of science, it does so with simple yet correct terms, not absurdities. Where non-biblical accounts of the formation of the universe and other scientific matters border on the ridiculous, the Scriptures nowhere are guilty of this. It is not what could be expected from a book written by men during pre-scientific times."[70] He's right. Men couldn't have done that. Neither could women. The Bible is not the result of natural inspiration. Its inspiration is divine.

Keep in mind that science has made some claims it has not yet proven that are contrary to the Bible. Evolution is one of those claims. If someone does create life in a test tube, it won't be evidence for evolution. It will only show how much intelligence it actually takes to create life. How many minds have been working on that project for how many years? But creating life in all of its forms was just another day at the office for God. Twern't no big thang.

Not only is the Bible scientifically accurate, it is also historically correct. We don't have to be concerned with the accuracy of either testament. They are right on.

The Historical Test

When the Old Testament was copied, letters were counted, both forward and backward, and measurements were taken from corner to corner to make sure spacing and punctuation were perfect. If a mistake was made, the page was thrown out, not corrected.

The discovery of the Dead Sea Scrolls confirmed how meticulous the Jewish scribes were in the copying of the texts. Only a few minor copyist errors were found between what we have in today's Bibles and the scrolls that were uncovered. No credibility problems resulted from the discoveries. Your Bible, if it's a legitimate translation, is miraculously close to the original. God has kept it intact.

Skeptics don't argue with the historicity of the Bible anymore. Dates, places, and occurrences are all right on the money and have been confirmed by archaeology. The Old Testament is historically correct. So is the New Testament.

Josh McDowell, in his classic *Evidence That Demands a Verdict*, reports on his findings regarding the New Testament:

> No other document of antiquity even begins to approach such numbers and attestation. In comparison, the *Iliad* by Homer is second with only 643 manuscripts that still survive. The first complete preserved text of Homer dates from the 13th century.
>
> There are now more than 5,300 known Greek manuscripts of the New Testament. Add over 10,000 Latin Vulgate and at least 9,300 other early versions and we have more than 24,000 manuscript copies of portions of the New Testament in existence today.[71]

John Warwick Montgomery says that "to be skeptical of the resultant text of the New Testament books is to allow all of classical antiquity to slip into obscurity, for no documents of the ancient period are as well attested bibliographically as the New Testament."[72]

Sir Frederic Kenyon reports that "the interval between the dates of original composition and the earliest extant evidence becomes so small as to be in fact negligible, and the last foundation for any doubt that the Scriptures have come down to us substantially as they were written has now been removed. Both the authenticity and the general integrity of the books of the New Testament may be regarded as finally established."[73]

The accuracy of the New Testament is confirmed by the variety of versions of manuscripts and by the contemporary historical writers of the time. McDowell and Stewart added their stamp of approval with the following endorsement:

> The history recorded in the Scriptures also proves to be accurate. As far as we have been able to check them out, the names, places and events mentioned in the Bible have been recorded accurately.[74]

Both the Old and New Testaments have been established to be historically correct, making the Bible accurate in its portrayal of times, dates, and places. Both testaments pass the historical test.

History offers more data than archaeology can confirm, but, archaeology is a way to confirm a portion of the Bible's historical accuracy and comprises our third test.

The Archaeological Test

For years there was no archaeological record of the Hittites. People called the Bible wrong. Then an archaeologist discovered their capital city, thousands of texts, the Hittite code, and we came to the realization that their empire had been vast.

Over the years skeptics maintained that Solomon was broke, that there was no such place as Sodom or Gomorrah, and that Belshazzar never existed. Solomon's wealth was confirmed between 1925 and 1934. Tablets have been uncovered confirming the existence of Sodom and Gomorrah. Belshazzar was for real. Archaeological discoveries provided the proof.

There are literally hundreds of volumes on this kind of stuff. Josh McDowell has read most of them and has compiled the opinions of the biggies in the field. His conclusion: "So far, the findings of archaeology have verified, and in no case disputed, historical points of the biblical record."[75]

The Bible passes the archaeological test with flying colors. Go to any archaeological dig in the Middle East. You'll find a searcher with a Bible in one hand and a shovel in the other. Why? The Bible is right, and whether you believe it or not doesn't change a thing. When God says, "It's over there," diggers have learned to look over there.

There are more tests than the triple test of trustworthiness. I like the next one most of all. I guess it's because I was raised as a bookmaker's kid.

The Test of Fulfilled Prophecy

In the olden days if you wanted to draw attention to yourself you would say, "Thus saith the Lord" and everybody would do that old E. F. Hutton routine and stop doin' what they were doin' to listen. People wanted to know what God said in those days. Note that I didn't say they wanted to *do* what He said. But they did want to know. I guess that's why everybody wanted to be a prophet. It could be a real power position.

There was a little problem with being a prophet, though. If you were wrong, they killed you. That's why few prophets collected social security. Only the ones God chose lived that long. But not all of God's prophets got old. If the people didn't like what God said, sometimes they would kill the prophet.

The folks found that God was never wrong. For example, God said the coastal city of Tyre would fall and never be rebuilt, and that its timbers and rubble would be thrown into the sea. "Fishermen will dry their nets where the city used to be," is what God said. But Tyre was a fortified city. "Impossible!" the people shouted. "Tyre will never fall."

Then along came Alexander the Great. He laid siege to Tyre, but the people escaped to a nearby island. Alexander brought in hundreds of slaves, tore down the town, chucked the debris into the water (forming a causeway), marched out to the island, and snuffed the folks. The foundation of the city of Tyre was scraped clean. Even though there are fresh water springs there (it's a perfect place for a city), you'll only find fishermen's nets drying in the sun. Why? Because God said so.

Prophets of God said Babylon would destroy Jerusalem. Come on, now! Girl Scouts aren't going to defeat Desert Storm troops. That's the way things were when the prophecy was made. But it happened. God said it would.

My favorite examples of the accuracy of God's Word are the Old Testament prophecies that were fulfilled with the coming of Christ. There are over three hundred, but many are fairly general. Sixty-one are quite specific:

- Christ would be betrayed by a friend, not a political leader or an acquaintance.

- The betrayal would be for silver, not gold.
- For thirty pieces, not forty.
- He would ride, not walk.
- Into Jerusalem, not some other city.
- On a donkey, not a horse.
- The donkey would be female, not male.

And on and on for sixty-one such prophecies.[76] Keep in mind that Christ had no control over His place, time, or manner of birth; His betrayal; manner of death; the people's reactions; the piercing of His side; or His burial. Yet, each prophecy was specifically proclaimed. At a specific point in time, in a town close to what was then considered the center of the world, one man defied the odds and made the prophecies of several authors who wrote at least twelve hundred years apart and at least four hundred years before it happened, come true.

A mathematician computed the odds of eight of the prophecies occurring by chance. The probability is one in ten to the seventeenth power. That's silver dollars two feet deep covering Texas, with one marked, and a blindfolded man walking in at random, bending over, and snagging the marked one on the first try.

The same math man ran the numbers on forty-eight prophecies occurring by chance. The number is one in ten to the 157th power. That's a cubic inch of electrons with one marked and getting it right on the first try. By the way, at 250 per minute, it would take nineteen million years to count one inch of electrons. Counting a cubic inch would require nineteen million times nineteen million times nineteen million, or 6.9 times ten to the twenty-first power years.[77]

I guess the mathematician quit after forty-eight prophecies. I can't imagine what sixty-one would do. But then, I had trouble visualizing eight.

Being a gambler's kid, that did it for me. I'm not going to bet against those kind of odds. Are you? If the Book that tells me about the coming together of sixty-one prophecies came together the way it came together and is still scientifically, historically, and archaeologically correct also tells me nice people really do go to hell, what am I gonna' do? Am I going to pick and choose what I'm going to believe and what I want to disbelieve? No! If the Book has always been right, then what is the likelihood that any of its basic themes are wrong? Not high. No, that's not strong enough language. How about impossible? The odds are too great to compute.

If a horse ran in ninety-nine races and won each time, would you bet against him in the hundredth?

You probably said, "No sir!"

But if you're a gambler you would reply, "It depends on the odds."

That's the way we are. We will bet against the odds if we think the return is good enough. That's how duped we are. We think that having our own way is worth going against those kind of odds. Frank Sinatra made "I Did It My Way" a popular song some years ago. It is the boastful life statement of a fool. He thinks what he's done and his legacy when he's gone will have been worth defying God. He bet against the odds and thinks he's won. And then comes death and eternity. Poor Frank.

Is the glitter of the world and living life your way worth betting on such long odds? I don't think so!

Don't go your way. You'll lose for sure. Trust God. Only then will you trust your Bible. Consider the following:

> If God is our ultimate authority and His character is flawless, and if He inspired the writers of

> Scripture to put down His thoughts while still allowing them freedom of personal expression, then the Bible [in its original form] is flawless and it becomes our ultimate authority—our only rule for faith and practice[78](brackets mine).

The Bible is a book you can count on. McDowell and Stewart conclude:

> The text of the Bible has been transmitted accurately. We may rest assured that what we have today is a correct representation of what was originally given. For example, there is more evidence for the reliability of the text of the New Testament as an accurate reflection of what was initially written than there is for any thirty pieces of classical literature put together.[79]

You might not understand it all right away, but it's trustworthy. Billy Graham's whole ministry changed when he made his leap of faith:

> I believe it is not possible to understand everything in the Bible intellectually. One day some years ago I decided to accept the Scriptures by faith. There were problems I could not reason through. When I accepted the Bible as the authoritative Word of God—by faith—I found immediately that it became a flame in my hand. That flame began to melt away unbelief in the hearts of many people and to move them to decide for Christ. The Word became a hammer, breaking up stony hearts and shaping men into the likeness of God. Did not God say, "I will make my words in thy mouth fire" (Jeremiah 5:14), and "Is not my word like as a fire? saith

> the Lord; and like a hammer that breaketh the rock in pieces?" (Jeremiah 23:29)?
> I found that I could take a simple outline, then put a number of Scripture quotations under each point, and God would use it mightily to cause men to make full commitment to Christ. I found that I did not have to rely upon cleverness, oratory, psychological manipulation, apt illustrations, or striking quotations from famous men. I began to rely more and more upon Scripture itself and God blessed it. I am convinced through my travels and experience that people all over the world are hungry to hear the Word of God.[80]

Add the proof of changed lives; the phenomenon of having a conscience; the calendar being split in two (B.C. and A.D.) by one person; Jesus Christ being the only name that's a swear word; the cross being the worldwide symbol for compassion; and the Bible being the best-selling, the most widely studied, and clearly the most closely scrutinized book in the history of the world; and you ought to have a clue that this deal is real.

As a people, Americans know the Bible is unique. As a nation we cherish it. But esteeming is different than following. To follow we have to know what it says. Although most homes have at least one Bible someplace, few people have read it enough to know what it says. Gallup confirms that statement: "Americans revere the Bible—but, by and large, they don't read it. And because they don't read it, they have become a nation of biblical illiterates."[81] Although four out of five Americans believe the Bible to be inspired by God, only 15 percent read it daily.[82] Gallup uses strong language when it comes to college graduates: "Particularly shocking is the lack of knowledge of the Bible among college graduates."[83] And he indicates that the statistics only will get worse. Three out of ten teenagers do not know why Easter is celebrated. Twenty percent who regularly attend religious services don't know any more about Easter than do those who don't.[84] It's hard to know what God wants you to do if you don't read His instruction manual.

I remember a Calvin and Hobbes cartoon. They were running around throwing a ball, sliding and hitting. It was baseball for two. Calvin asked Hobbes, "Are you out, or am I?"

Hobbes reply was classic: "It depends which game we are playing."

Since so few have read the rule book, most people have decided to make up their own rules and play their own game. In their book *The Day America Told the Truth*, Patterson and Kim discuss the new moral authority in America. Their conclusion? It's you:

> It's the wild, wild West all over again in America, but it's wilder and woollier this time. You are the law in this country. Who says so? You do, pardner.
>
> In the 1950s and even in the early 1960s, there was something much closer to a moral consensus in America. It was mirrored in a parade of moralizing family TV programs: "Ozzie and Harriet," "Father Knows Best," "Donna Reed," "Leave It to Beaver," and even "Bonanza."
>
> There is absolutely no moral consensus at all in the 1990s. Everyone is making up their own personal moral codes—their own Ten Commandments.
>
> Here are ten extraordinary commandments for the 1990s. These are real commandments, the

rules that many people actually live by. (The percentage of people who live by each commandment is included.)

1. I don't see the point in observing the Sabbath (77%).
2. I will steal from those who won't really miss it (74%).
3. I will lie when it suits me, so long as it doesn't cause any real damage (64%).
4. I will drink and drive if I feel that I can handle it. I know my limit (56%).
5. I will cheat on my spouse—after all, given the chance, he or she will do the same (53%).
6. I will procrastinate at work and do absolutely nothing about one full day in every five. It's standard operating procedure (50%).
7. I will use recreational drugs (41%).
8. I will cheat on my taxes—to a point (30%).
9. I will put my lover at risk of disease. I sleep around a bit, but who doesn't (31%)?
10. [Author's note—the tenth one was too tacky. I left it out.]

Almost all of us have highly individualized moral menus like that today. We decide what's right and wrong. Most Americans have no respect for what the law says.[85]

Most people don't treat the Bible as if it were God's personal word to them. But regardless of how people respond to it, the Bible is God's revelation to us. It has to be. The odds against it are just too great. The chance that it might not be is too remote. Being God's Word makes what it says about Christ to be truth.

Is Jesus Christ for Real?

> In 1978, 78 percent of Americans said Jesus was God or the Son of God; this increased to 84 percent in 1988. In 1978, 60 percent of Americans said they had made a personal commitment to Jesus; this rose to 66 percent in 1988. These increases are highly significant because basic beliefs of this kind are generally very slow to change. Believing women went from 81 to 85 percent. Believing men rose from 75 to 79 percent. Fifty-one percent of Americans said that at some time in their lives they had encouraged others to believe in Jesus or accept Him as their Savior, and 62 percent have no doubts that Christ will return to Earth someday.[86]
>
> So says George Gallup.

How can more people identify with Christ but end up with fewer people embracing their Bibles? The bottom line is: identification is different from commitment.

We have a parallel problem to deal with here. If the Bible is real, then all that it tells us about Jesus is true. If the Bible is wrong, then the object of the Christian faith, Jesus Christ, becomes suspect. Consider MacArthur's conclusion:

> Can you believe in Christ but not in the authority and infallibility of the Bible? You can try, but it will leave you on the horns of a very real dilemma, and here is why: If you say you believe in Christ but doubt the Bible's truthfulness, you are being inconsistent and even irrational. Christ endorsed the Bible as true and authoritative. If you give Christ a place of honor and authority in your life,

it follows that to be consistent you have to give Scripture that same honor and authority.[87]

Continuing, he said, "The authority and authenticity of Christ, and the Scriptures, stand or fall together."[88] In other words, you have to embrace both to embrace either one. But trying to embrace one without the other is to reject both.

Let's take a look to see if there are good reasons to believe Jesus Christ is real.

My Favorite Reasons for Jesus Being Real

I've already used up my favorites. There are the three biggies. Certainly, having one man fulfill sixty-one specific prophecies is significant. It's the singular piece of data that's affected my faith the most. The second is the liar, lunatic, or Lord argument. That argument has greatly strengthened my position on Christ. Finally, the Bible hasn't been wrong anyplace else. Therefore, I don't believe it's wrong about who Jesus is. Those three have had the greatest influence on me.

The effect of Christian missionaries around the world and the countless changed lives can't be overlooked. Yet some still doubt that Jesus even lived, while others agree that He lived, but there was nothing supernatural or miraculous about Him. Geisler and Brooks take us back to the reliability of the Bible for their argument:

1. Gospel records were written by eyewitnesses within forty years of the events described. This gives their account credibility and assures a fair degree of accuracy.
2. The Bible is not one account of those events, but at least four accounts which agree in the main facts.

3. The account given in the New Testament agrees with the evidence from secular and Jewish historians of the first and second centuries.
4. The Bible has proven to be remarkably accurate in what it says about the ancient world. For example, in citing thirty-two countries, fifty-four cities, nine islands, and several rulers, Luke never made a mistake.

So there is no reason that the New Testament should not be accepted as a reliable historical document which gives us valuable information about the life and death of Jesus of Nazareth.[89]

What are the odds of a myth affecting the world like Jesus Christ has and continues to do? Only the kinds of people who don't believe in Australia because they haven't been there would doubt the reality of Christ. He lived, of that we are sure.

Dale Foreman wrote a fascinating book titled *Crucify Him: A Lawyer Looks at the Trial of Jesus.*[90] Applying an attorney's expertise, he spends 211 pages developing his case. Exhibit A contains 147 facts. Exhibit A2 has one hundred facts. A3 has forty-four. Exhibit B contains a time line and Exhibit C contains data from associated writings. It's quite complete. His conclusion: Jesus is for real!

Consider Christ's credentials. Paul Little organized them as follows: His moral character coincided with His claims. He demonstrated a power over natural forces which could belong only to God, the Author of these forces. He demonstrated the Creator's power over sickness and disease. Jesus' supreme credential to authenticate His claim to deity was His resurrection from the dead. Finally, we know that Christ is God because we can experience Him in this century.[91]

Those are some mighty fine qualifications. But the whole of Christianity still pivots on the singular hinge of Easter and all that it means. Fulfilled prophecy, calendars, swear words, and arguments are noteworthy, but it's meaningless if Christ didn't conquer death.

Did Christ Rise from the Dead?

If He overcame death for Himself, then I can believe He overcame it for me. But if death got the best of Him, then I am without hope. We observe Good Friday, but we celebrate Easter. Why? Anybody can die. Everybody will. But only one person ever walked away from death and never had to die again.

A thorough examination of the resurrection is not within the confines of this book, but more than five hundred people saw Jesus walking around for forty days after He rose. Paul wrote about it around A.D. 56 and indicated there were plenty of people who had seen Jesus after the crucifixion who were still alive at the time the apostle did his writing.

That Jesus died is not arguable. Medical doctors agree that when the spear pierced Him, Christ's blood had already separated. That only happens when you're good and dead. Luke's description of the event is strong evidence that Christ died. So much for the swoon theory.

Did someone steal His body? Not the Romans; they had no reason. They wanted peace and leaving the body alone would have produced it. Not the Jews; they wanted to quench this resurrection business. A body left alone would have done that. Not the disciples; all but one would later be killed for something they knew to be untrue. That's not gonna' happen. Someone would have squealed.

McDowell and Stewart present a conclusion and a great story about a researcher:

> The historical evidence is more than sufficient to satisfy the curiosity of the honest inquirer. This can be seen not only by the positive defense that can be made for the case for the resurrection, but also by the lack of any evidence for an alternative explanation. The theories attempting to give an alternative explanation to the resurrection take more faith to believe than the resurrection itself.
>
> Frank Morrison, who was an agnostic journalist, attempted to write a book refuting the resurrection of Christ. After much investigation, his opinions changed and he became a believer in Jesus Christ. This is how Morrison described what happened to him:
>
> "This study is in some ways so unusual and provocative that the writer thinks it desirable to state here very briefly how the book came to take its present form. In one sense it could have taken no other, for it is essentially a confession, the inner story of a man who originally set out to write one kind of book and found himself compelled by the sheer force of circumstances to write another. It is not that the facts altered, for they are recorded imperishably in the monuments and in the pages of human history. But the interpretation to be put on the facts underwent a change" (*Who Moved the Stone?* Grand Rapids, Mich.: Zondervan, 1971, preface).[92]

If you mess with the Master, you're gonna' get mastered. If you take a good look at Jesus Christ, you'll probably invite Him to be the boss of your life. That's what happened to

Frank Morrison. It was the same for Josh McDowell, the apologetics author I've referenced frequently in this chapter. And C.S. Lewis too (the British author who wrote *Mere Christianity*, *The Chronicles of Narnia*, and numerous other works), and countless others as well. When the facts come together there is only one conclusion to be made—the whole deal is real. I hope that is your conclusion. It should be, unless you're a long-shot gambler.

In this chapter I wanted to share a few of the apologetics that have been meaningful to me. (Don't get confused by the word *apologetic*. I'm not apologizing for anything. It's a word that means "defending the faith in a formal presentation.") So much has been written over the years. My desire was to convey a few of my favorites.

There shouldn't be any doubt about the purpose of this book by now. Let me summarize. The odds strongly suggest the following conclusions:

God is real.
The Bible is real.
Jesus Christ is real.
Hell is real.
Heaven is real.
The whole deal is real.
You're gonna' die.
There is nothing more valuable than a soul.
Nice people really do go to hell.

Did concepts collide for you?

Do you believe that the whole deal is real?

Does your life reflect your belief?

Oops! It's your move. What are you bettin' on?

Do you have a firmer faith? Perhaps saving faith is the result. If either outcome occurred from reading this book, I'm thrilled, and the hours spent together will have been worth it.

May God bless you as you walk with Him. Finish well.

Personal Note

If God has used this book to make a difference in your life, drop me a note. It would be an encouragement.

I also have a monthly newsletter. My speaking schedule is always included, so you'll know if I'm ever in your area. Indicate on your note if you'd like to receive "Obedient Thoughts."

If you are interested in audio tapes of this series or other messages I've done, let me know. Do the same for any of my books you can't find in your local bookstore. I'll send you a price list so you can order what you want.

Finally, if you need a speaker for your church or a conference, write or call:

Jay Carty
Yes! Ministries
1033 Newton Rd.
Santa Barbara, CA 93103
(805) 962-7579

Other books written by Jay Carty include:

Counterattack: Taking Back Ground Lost to Sin
A practical guide to spiritual warfare.
(Yes! Ministries)

Something's Fishy:
Getting Rid of the Carp in Your Life
A book for those who are lukewarm.
(Yes! Ministries)

Developing Your Natural Talents

A guide leading you to the discovery of your God-given natural talents and how to negotiate their use into work and ministry. (NavPress)

Only Tens Go to Heaven

A booklet (thirty pages) presenting the gospel message (including repentance) in words and cartoons. (Yes! Ministries)

Endnotes

1. Billy Graham, *Facing Death* (Waco, Tex.: Word Books, 1987), 57.

2. See Isaiah 59:1-2, Ephesians 2:1, Revelation 21:4, and Mark 9:44.

3. It is possible that a resurrected "new body" will free those in heaven from the restriction of time. Like God, we might be able to be in multiple places at once. Since we will still be restricted to our new bodies that is unlikely. But it certainly won't be the case for those in hell, because they will be restricted to wherever that place is and therefore will probably have an awareness of time passing—eternally. Of course, God may eliminate time altogether. He created it, so He can dispense with it. I'm just guessing that He won't for those in hell.

4. Tony Campolo "Christian Camping in the '90s," audio-taped message at Hume Lake Christian Camps, 1991.

5. I'm going to break the rules of writing by not capitalizing the name of satan. I choose not to honor him in any way.

6. Donald E. Sloat, *The Dangers of Growing Up in a Christian Home* (Nashville, Tenn.: Thomas Nelson, Inc., 1986), 112.

7. John H. Gerstner, *Repent or Perish* (Ligonier, Penn.: Gloria Publications, 1990), 13.

8. Ibid., 23.

9. Ibid., 28.

10. Ibid., 29.

11. George Gallup, Jr. and Jim Castelli, *The People's Religion* (New York, N.Y.: MacMillan Publishing Company, 1989), 45-59.

12. James Patterson and Peter Kim. *The Day America Told the Truth* (New York: Prentice Hall Press, 1991), 204.

13. Graham, *Facing Death*, 36.

14. John Stott, *Evangelical Essentials* (Downers Grove, Ill.: Inter-Varsity Press, 1989); Philip Hughes, *The True Image* (Grand Rapids, Mich.: Eerdmans Publishing Co., 1989); Edward William Fudge, *The Fire That Consumes* (Houston, Tex.: Providential Press, 1983); and others.

15. Gerstner, *Repent or Perish*, 62.

16. Graham, *Facing Death*, 34.

17. Merril C. Tenney, ed., *Zondervan Pictorial Encyclopedia of the Bible*, vol. 4, (Grand Rapids, Mich.: Zondervan, 1974), 956.

18. Lewis Sperry Chafer, *Systematic Theology*, vol. IV, (Dallas, Tex.: Dallas Seminary Press, 1947), 429.

19. Although their opinion is in the vast minority, a few commentators do not believe the compartment theory is correct. Some believe the Old Testament saints went straight to heaven. Moses and Elijah being with Christ at the Transfiguration suggest they were in heaven, not Hades. And Christ told the thief on the cross next to Him that they would be in paradise that very day, not Hades. The argument is academic. Moses and Elijah could have come from the penthouse and Christ could have done His thing in Hades before the thief died. It doesn't matter who is correct, since we all agree that those who die in Christ today are in heaven.

20. Tim LaHaye, *How to Study Bible Prophecy for Yourself* (Eugene, Ore.: Harvest House Publishers, 1976), 181.

21. Ibid., 184.

22. Ibid., 185.

23. Kennedy, 75.

24. Ross French, "Playing 'Keep Away' with God," *Daily Nexus*, University of California at Santa Barbara, April 11, 1991.

(University newspaper article written by a senior English major/sports writer.)

25. Merrill C. Tenney, gen. ed., *The Zondervan Pictorial Bible Dictionary* (Grand Rapids, Mich.: Zondervan Publishing House, 1963), 497.

26. John MacArthur, "Heaven" tape series, 1987. Order from: Grace to You, P.O. Box 4000, Panorama City, California 91412. (Note—My thanks to Dr. MacArthur. This series was terrific. I relied on it heavily in the writing of this chapter.)

27. Ibid. (The quotation is not exact. I transcribed it from the tape and adapted it for copy.)

28. Kennedy. p. 66.

29. I have asked this question for almost ten years during my travels around the country speaking in churches, camps, and retreats. Eighty percent of the respondents place themselves in third soil.

30. Jay Carty, *Something's Fishy* (Portland, Ore.: Multnomah Press, 1990).

31. I am not suggesting that this person lost his salvation. This one never had it in the first place. Nor is this person a backslider. Backsliders are third soil.

32. Unless your heart has been hardened, like Pharaoh who had become apostate.

33. For a discussion on this subject, see my first book, *Counterattack* (Portland, Ore.: Multnomah Press, 1988).

34. Watterson, "Calvin and Hobbes" comic strip, owner of copyright, Newspaper Syndication. December 23, 1990.

35. George Will, "The Season of '41" *Newsweek*, 8 April 1991, 68.

36. Lewis Sperry Chafer, *Systematic Theology*, vol. IV, 430.

37. Jay Carty, *Only Tens Go to Heaven* (San Bernardino, Calif.: Churches Alive, year?)., This booklet is about the size of a long Hallmark greeting card and is around thirty pages long. Each page contains cartoons as well as concepts. There is Moses with a tablet under each arm saying, "Betcha' can't break just one." The capper is the picture of God in a judge's hat wearing a shirt with an Olympic logo on the pocket, holding up a "10" sign saying, "I'll give her a ten

because she's a friend of my Son." The booklet is a complete presentation of the gospel and it includes repentance. It's for your off-the-wall friends who don't know Christ. Personally, I think every guest bathroom in the country ought to have one on the back of the toilet. The booklet takes about ten minutes to read. Two of the concepts in *Tens* are the righteousness scale and the jump of the Grand Canyon.

38. Ron Carlson was speaking at Hume Lake Christian Camps on July 7, 1991.

39. J. Robertson McQuilkin, *The Narrow Way*, 131.

40. Don Richardson, *Eternity in Their Hearts* (Ventura, Calif.: Regal Books, 1978), 9-71.

41. Ibid., 73-109.

42. Ibid., 128-129.

43. Ibid., 155-156.

44. I like the New American Standard version for this passage.

45. Some believe that the baptism of repentance applied for the generation of which John was a part and ended thereafter. It is not a strong argument biblically.

46. McQuilkin, *The Narrow Way*, 133-134.

47. I do not have a source for the story and am not sure it's true. Someone thought it was from a Wycliffe publication. Another thought it came from one of Don Richardson's books. I couldn't find it in either. But it doesn't matter. It still illustrates what God is capable of doing if He chooses.

48. "What a Life Is Worth: U.S. Seeks a Price" *U.S. News & World Report*, 16 September 1985, 58.

49. Ibid.

50. Ibid.

51. Ibid.

52. Carlson message, July 7, 1991.

53. If that's a problem for you, let me recommend John Bradley and Jay Carty, *Unlocking Your Sixth Suitcase* (Colorado Springs, Colo.: NavPress, 1991).

54. Merrill C. Tenney, ed., *Zondervan Pictorial Encyclopedia of the Bible*, vol. 3 (Grand Rapids, Mich.: Zondervan, 1974), 117.

55. Richard Wurmbrandt, *Tortured for Christ* (Middlebury, Ind.:

Living Sacrifice Books, 1986).

56. I am referring to hell, the lake of fire, not the pit where satan is to be confined for a thousand years.

57. If you need help brainstorming to validate your talents or to discover how to use them, see John Bradley and Jay Carty, *Unlocking Your Sixth Suitcase* (Colorado Springs, Colo.: NavPress, 1991).

58. In *Counterattack* I demonstrate a technique for doing this called a polar bear alert.

59. Remember, this is the big-time apostle Paul who is struggling. So you will probably struggle, too.

60. If we confess our sins, he is faithful and just and will forgive us our sins and purify us from all unrighteousness.

61. Gallup, *The People's Religion*, 56.

62. Ron Carlson, Hume Lake tape, 1991.

63. David Jeremiah. "Facing Transitions in Life—Joshua 3," cassette tape, Hume Lake, June 17, 1990.

64. Winkie Pratney, *The Holy Bible: Wholly True* (Lindale, Tex.: Pretty Good Printing, 1979).

65. John F. MacArthur, Jr., *Why Believe the Bible?* (Glendale, Calif.: Regal Books, 1978), 41.

66. Ibid., 52.

67. Ibid., 57.

68. Josh McDowell and Don Stewart, *Reasons Skeptics Should Consider Christianity* (Wheaton, Ill.: Tyndale House Publishers, Inc., 1988), 77.

69. Ibid., 21.

70. McDowell and Stewart, *Reasons Skeptics Should Consider Christianity*, 76.

71. Josh McDowell, *Evidence That Demands a Verdict* (San Bernardino, Calif.: Here's Life Publishers, Inc., 1979), 39-40.

72. Ibid., 40.

73. Ibid., 41.

74. McDowell and Stewart, *Reasons Skeptics Should Consider Christianity*, 75.

75. Josh McDowell and Don Stewart, *Answers to Tough Questions* (Wheaton, Ill.: Tyndale House Publishers, Inc., 1980), 35.

76. McDowell, *Evidence That Demands a Verdict*, 144-166. This is the best listing of which I am aware and is must reading.

77. Ibid., 167.

78. MacArthur, *Why Believe the Bible?*, 9.

79. McDowell and Stewart, *Reasons Skeptics Should Consider Christianity*, 74-75.

80. Billy Graham, "The Authority of Scripture," *Decision*, June 1963.

81. Gallup, *The People's Religion*, 60.

82. Ibid., 60.

83. Ibid., 60.

84. Ibid., 60.

85. Patterson, *The Day America Told the Truth*, 25-26.

86. Gallup, *The People's Religion*, 63.

87. MacArthur, *Why Believe the Bible?*, 44.

88. Ibid., 51.

89. Norman Geisler and Ronald Brooks, *When Skeptics Ask* (Wheaton, Ill.: Victor Books, 1990), 103.

90. Dale Foreman, *Crucify Him* (Grand Rapids, Mich.: Zondervan Publishing House, 1990).

91. Paul Little, *Know Why You Believe* (Wheaton, Ill.: Victor Books, 1988), 37-40.

92. McDowell and Stewart, *Answers to Tough Questions*, 82.

Study Guide

Introduction to the Study Guide

We have suggested questions to look for in each chapter as you read. We call them *Something to look for as you read.* (Catchy, huh?) *Look over these questions first* and then check the answers as you come to them in the chapter. Note these answers in the margin simply by recording the number of the question or highlighting the answer with a highlighter as you read. This will give you a reference point when you go over the chapter to discuss it.

The second set of questions are more open-ended. We call these *Something to talk about.* (Aren't you just overwhelmed with all this creativity?) These are to talk about after you have read the chapter. We've tried to provide about an hour's worth.

If you are reading this book alone (i.e., not studying it with a group) we suggest that you write out the answers to each question. I know, that sounds a lot like school, but it is a good discipline and will help you to gain a greater grasp of the material.

If, on the other hand, you are studying this in a group, these questions will form the basis of discussion.

For Group Leaders

We suggest that you assign one chapter per session. Ask each participant to read the chapter using the *Something to look for as you read* questions as a guide through the chapter. Have them mark the answers to each question as they go. After they have read the chapter in this way, then have each participant read the *Something to talk about* questions and be prepared to discuss them in the group meeting.

Feel free to use any question you want in the group discussion. You are not limited to just the *Something to talk about* questions. This is the beauty of being the facilitator of a small group. You can guide your group into those areas where they can get the most help because you know the needs of your group better than anyone else.

There is a strong argument in this book for readers to accept Jesus Christ as their personal Savior. Don't bypass this opportunity to face your group with this challenge. Do not assume that they are all already Christians. One of the enemy's deceptions is to allow us to think we are Christians when we really are not. Press your group for a commitment at the appropriate time.

Introduction and Chapter 1
Why Dread Death?

Something to look for as you read

1. Who was the player Jay went to see?
2. What other schools were after him?
3. What scared Jay that night?
4. What makes death scary?
5. How many puffs did it take to bring the woman back?
6. Where did Jay first look death in the face?
7. Who were the two people who didn't have to die?
8. Who were the most righteous people in the Old Testament?
9. Who were the people Jesus raised from the dead?

Something to talk about

1. Discuss the importance of considering probabilities (odds) when making decisions. Include the concepts of upside potential

versus downside risk. Then apply your conclusions to the concepts of heaven and hell.

2.Why would a person risk spending eternity in hell? Consider the reasons.

3. Explain Paul's attitude toward death. How did he arrive at this attitude and what are its ingredients? Give scripture verses to support your answer

4. What makes us fear death? List as many fear-causing things as you can.

5. Discuss the implications of Billy Graham's statement: "It becomes increasingly evident that the way we view death determines, to a surprising degree, the way we live our lives."

Chapter 2
What Kind of Dead Are You?

Something to look for as you read

1. What are the three kinds of death?
2. What constitutes physical death?
3. What constitutes spiritual death?
4. What are the consequences of a "Daddy no-no?"
5. What is the only solution to spiritual death?
6. What is spiritual suicide?
7. What constitutes eternal death?

Something to talk about

1. How does the concept of different kinds of death reconcile reported out-of-body experiences as you understand them and Hebrews 9:27? Might there be exceptions? Talk about it.

2. Why are babies born spiritually dead?

3. What are the requirements to move from spiritual death to spiritual life, and what are the benefits of such a move?

4. If the hell of the Bible is not literal, why would the real hell be even worse?

5. Why is man's greatest need the need to know his greatest need?

Chapter 3
Where to Next—Hell?

Something to look for as you read

1. According to the Bible, people spend eternity in one of two places. What are these places, and what determines where we'll go?

2. What are three biblically sound reasons for coming to Christ?

3. What are the two facts quoted from *Something's Fishy?*

4. What is generally our first response to bad news?

5. Where did the righteous Old Testament person go when he died? How about the unrighteous Old Testament person? Or Jesus?

6. What suggests that there will be degrees of punishment in hell?

7. Who rules hell?

Something to talk about

1. Discuss the pros and cons of scare tactics versus a gospel of love.

2. What are your responses to the statistics on page 52?

3. What are alternative theories presented by people who deny the reality of hell, and why are they unacceptable?

4. Consider the summary of hell on pages 70-71. Which are the most distasteful to you and why?

Chapter 4
Where to Next—Heaven?

Something to look for as you read

1. What was the miracle that happened to Paul in Acts 14?

2. What are the three heavens?

3. Where is heaven?

4. What is the buzzword from Princess Bride?

5. Who is the standard you must compare yourself to when you claim to be a good person?

6. When you stand before God, why won't you need a lawyer? What will you need?

Something to talk about

1. List the misconceptions of the college student's letter and state how you would answer them.
2. Describe what it will be like to live in heaven.
3. Play the game called "Heaven is better than . . . ."
4. Compile a list of possible reasons why God didn't want Paul to tell about all he had seen.
5. What are the first five things you'll do in heaven if you get the chance? Be as honest as you can and tell why.

Chapter 5
Which Place? There Are Clues in Your Clods

Something to look for as you read

1. What determines the value of dirt?
2. List the four kinds of soil in Matthew 13:3-9.
3. Which kind of soil do most Christians consider themselves to be?
4. What verse answers the question about the salvation of Dirt #1?
5. What evidence is there that Jay is a basketball player?
6. What is it that distinguishes a person's posture with God?
7. Why is it so hard to be fruit inspectors?
8. Where do Dirt #3 people end up?
9. What is the badge of a Dirt #4 person?
10. What are two "biggies" when it comes to saying no to God?

Something to talk about

1. What are the things Jay pulls out of the bag and what do they represent?
2. Is Dirt #2 going to heaven or hell? Support your answer.
3. Why is an understanding of Dirt #3 so important?
4. Discuss the four kinds of dirt and give current examples of each.
5. Explain the difference between discipline and punishment.

Chapter 6
Who Goes Where and Why?

Something to look for as you read

1. Why can't onions go to heaven?

2. What happens to an onion that is wrapped in the handiwrap of Jesus Christ?

3. What is the standard for measuring time?

4. How many baseball players would be in the Hall of Fame if they were measured against the standard?

5. Using the baseball analogy, what are the two ways to get into heaven?

6. What three words are defined in this chapter and what are their definitions?

Something to talk about

1. Set up your own righteousness scale and put yourself on it.

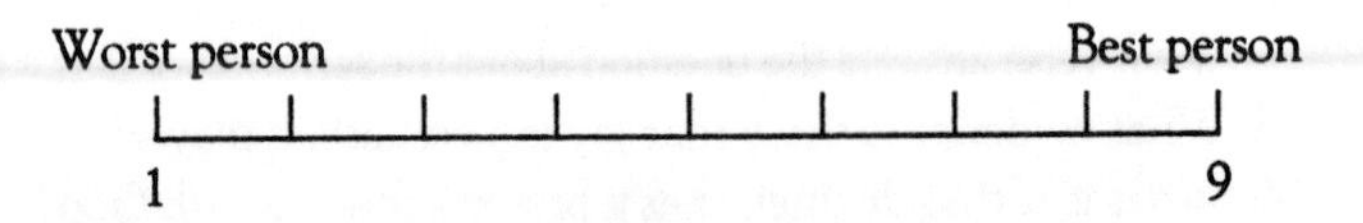

Where does God draw His line? Talk about comparisons.

2. Discuss how good you have to be to be considered good.

3. What are differences in the concepts of justice in the movie and the curfew story?

4. Why do I not want justice from God?

5. Using the Grand Canyon illustration and the scale above, share your position on the scale and where you are spiritually right now.

Chapter 7
What about the Ones Who Never Hear?

Something to look for as you read

1. What are God's three kinds of revelation?

2. How does God answer the statement, "But I didn't know?"

3. What are the seven components of God's progressive revelation?

4. In the C.S. Lewis story, why was it necessary to believe Lucy? Why was that belief so difficult?

5. Does God make exceptions? Name some.

6. What was Peter's answer when asked who Jesus was?

7. What is your answer to the question, "Who is Jesus?"

Something to talk about

1. Is it possible for people to get to heaven if they never heard about Jesus? Why or why not?

2. How does the fate of those who never heard influence your situation? Explain your answer.

3. Discuss your response to the McQuilkin quote.

Chapter 8
What Would You Pay for a Soul?

Something to look for as you read

1. Which is more valuable, a life or a soul?

2. How do you determine the value of something?

3. List the variables that determine the value of a life.

4. What was the value of a soul at the fundraising banquet for the conference center near Seattle?

5. Will most people pay more for a life or for a soul? Why?

6. From God's perspective, how does supply and demand, economics, and relationship affect the worth of a soul?

7. What criteria does God use in determining the worth of a soul?

8. What sins did Jesus not die for?

Something to talk about

1. How is the value of a life determined among your friends, family, church, etc.?

2. What are the "unpardonable sin" and the "sin unto death"? Do they disqualify us from heaven? Why or why not?

3. What are the dangers of repeating a sin over and over?

4. What is the net result of you understanding the worth of a soul?

5. How have you applied the value variables to the people God has put in your life? How does this understanding impact you?

Chapter 9
Makin' Sense?

Something to look for as you read

1. Why did Scott push his friend out of the boat?

2. What are Jay's three motives for writing this book?

3. What was the most beautiful music heard by Richard Wurmbrandt?

4. What was the greatest day in John Carty's basketball career?

5. What relationship does belief have with commitment?

6. In the story about the dam that burst, what difference did the boy make? How about the man?

Something to talk about

1. How can a person get to the place where he can legitimately "toss someone in the river"?

2. Which is more difficult: To face a frontal assault by Satan or to face his subtle temptations?

3. Identify several opportunities open to you where you can "bloom where you're planted."

4. Have any concepts collided in your mind during the reading of this book? Discuss your response.

Chapter 10
The Last Button on Jeb's Shirt

Something to look for as you read

1. What impact does my belief have on truth?

2. What mistake did Maurice and Jeff make?

3. What was the problem with the lost family in the story told by Don Snow?

4. What word characterizes the father in Don's story?

5. What does the UCLA research project prove?

6. Why did the Philistines continue to worship Dagon?

7. What was the young girl's problem in the story about the weekend away?

8. What lies ahead for you if you receive Christ? If you don't?

Something to talk about

1. Compare the two stories (Maurice and Jeff with the story Don Snow told). What are the similarities? What are the differences? What suggestions would you give to each?

2. Discuss the changes that took place in the lives of those who encountered Jesus. Relate the stories of others whom you know that encountered Jesus.

3. Why are fence sitters uncomfortable?

4. How is the phone like the Holy Spirit?

5. What more do you need to know before you can make a decision for Christ? Where are you right now? What do you think about the suggested prayer in this chapter? Is there any reason you cannot pray it right now?

Chapter 11
Why the Whole Deal Is Real

Something to look for as you read

1. What is the law of the odds?

2. What is the law of the sail squirrel?

3. What does time do to the probability of chance?

4. How does Israel's forty years wandering in the wilderness argue for the existence of God?

5. Why does the unity of theme in the Bible prove it to be a supernatural book?

6. What is the scientific test, and how does the Bible fare in this test?

7. What is the historical test, and how does the Bible fare in this test?

8. What is the archaeological test, and how does the Bible fare in this test?

9. What is the test of fulfilled prophecy, and how does the Bible fare in this test?

Something to talk about

1. Discuss the reasons for believing that God is real.
2. Discuss the reasons for believing that the Bible is real.
3. Discuss the reasons for believing that Jesus is real.
4. Discuss the reasons for believing that Jesus rose from the dead.
5. What are the odds on the whole deal being real? What difference does that make to you?

HERE ARE TWO EXCERPTS FROM JAY CARTY'S OTHER BOOKS:

BASIC TRAINING: CRUCIAL CONCEPTS FOR WAR

An excerpt from
Counterattack:
Taking Back Ground Lost to Sin

I have a friend, Don Snow, who is retired from the Army. He finished his tour in Viet Nam and has some great stories. My favorite is about his first night mission.

Upon entering a village one particularly black and inky night, Don heard breathing on the other side of a fence. When he took a step, a step was taken on the other side. When he stopped, it stopped. And so it went, the full length of the fence.

As Don approached the end of the barrier, he flipped the safety on his M-2 carbine and set it on automatic. His heart beat wildly, tension sweat soaked through his shirt, and the pit of his stomach ached with emotion. There was no way to know how many enemy Vietcong were on the other side. But Don was ready for whatever might happen. He was a well trained veteran.

As he got to the end of the fence, he took as deep a breath as he could and held it. He still heard breathing on the other side, but the steps had stopped. Then with all the strength, quickness, and agility he had, my friend coiled and sprang around the corner with his carbine blazing.

To his surprise he had just killed the biggest pig in Viet Nam.

The poor hog never knew what hit him. For that matter the animal didn't even know there was a war going on, and until that moment didn't care.

Most people are like that pig. They don't know there is a literal war going on, and they don't care.

God's Word talks about war raging in the supernatural heavenlies. Whether we realize it or not, each of us also lives in a combat zone. A battle rages on earth as well as in supernatural dimensions.

Satan's strategy in the war is twofold: (1) keep non-believers from believing, and (2) keep believers powerless in sin. He uses lies, accusations, and confusion as his primary weapons for occupying the ground he takes from us and for keeping us on the defensive.

However, we do have protective armor and an arsenal of our own. We'll be discussing three concepts you need to know before counterattacking the enemy in battle: éclairs in your refrigerator, polar bear alerts, and how aliens get their feet in the door.

ÉCLAIRS IN YOUR REFRIGERATOR

Let's assume you're on a diet, but on the way home you walk by your favorite bakery. The pangs of hunger are overwhelming and at that moment you would rather be fat than hungry, so you go in and buy two chocolate éclairs. Upon arriving home you're feeling guilty and somewhat defeated so you put the éclairs in the refrigerator and go into the living room where you kneel and pray, "Oh God, help me not to eat those chocolate éclairs."

How much power was in that prayer? The answer is to be found in the analysis in your heart. Why did you put the éclairs in the refrigerator?

To save them, of course.

You wanted to make sure the pastries wouldn't spoil until you could justify eating them. In other words, *you had already made up your mind to live against your prayers*. When your heart doesn't match the words of your prayers you are double-minded, you have éclairs in your refrigerator. Éclairs stifle the power of prayer.

POLAR BEAR ALERT

Is temptation sin? Don't respond too quickly. Before you decide, think back to last Sunday in church. You were sitting there with your Bible open, listening intently to the speaker, when out of the clear blue sky a flock of wild thoughts flew over and some of them circled and landed—you thought about "that." Is that sin?

Doing "that" would be a sin, but thinking "that" isn't—yet. Don't feel defeated with the first thought. You have a sin nature, you have to endure direct, frontal assault ("fiery darts") from the enemy. Therefore, it shouldn't be surprising that improper images come to mind. So, the first thought is not sin—but you're close.

If you make the conscious decision to dwell on an impure thought, embellish it, and let it run for a while, you just sinned.

When your imagination comes in conflict with your will, it's your imagination that usually prevails. That's why you need to learn how to have a polar bear alert.

Here's how.

Go in the corner and don't think of a white polar bear.

What did you think of? A polar bear, that's right. Not just because you're rebellious. You are, but not just because of that. It's because you didn't have anything else to think about.

This time, let's try it this way. Make the white polar bear cause you to think of a pink elephant. The white polar bear is going to be the catalyst generating the image of a pink elephant in your mind. Ready?

Go in the corner and don't think of a white polar bear. What did you think of? Did you say a pink elephant?

Wrong. First you thought of a white polar bear, and then a pink elephant.

The difference between the second time and the first time is subtle but it's very important: *The white polar bear didn't stay in your head as long when you had a pink elephant to think about.* That's a crucial concept if we call temptation the white polar bear, and if we call pink elephants the things of God.

If you practice substitute thinking, you're not going to sin. You will have used temptation as a catalyst to make you think of godly things. So, whenever you have a polar bear alert, make yourself think of 2 Corinthians 10:5. *You'll need to memorize it:* "We are destroying speculations and every lofty thing raised up against the knowledge of God, and we are taking every thought captive to the obedience of Christ."

ALIENS CAN GET A FOOT IN THE DOOR

A person who makes provision for sin opens the way to the influence of satan. They offer a geographical place for the enemy's clout. That is the nature of the word translated "foothold" or "opportunity" in Ephesians 4:27.

When you willingly stick your face into God's face, say "NO!" and refuse to repent, it's as if you took a wood-splitting maul (a fat axe) and drove it into your chest, but it didn't break the skin. Instead it left a wedge-like divot—a place for critters to hide. That newly created cavity in your sternum is a foothold. It's the result of ground you gave to the enemy. Chronic sin produces openings for our adversary.

To help you grasp this principle, I'd like you to visualize a tiny "Aliens" kind of character with a strange shaped head, a pot belly, skinny little legs, lizardlike skin, and suction cup fingers. You can see the little guy sitting in there, and it was you who made room for him. Actually, the alien could look like lots of things, and may not even look like anything at all. But he represents an enemy of Christ, and he's under the direction of the devil himself, assigned to the place of opportunity you provided because you didn't take care of your sin properly.

When you finally decided to repent from your long-term sin and claimed 1 John 1:9 ("If we confess our sins, he is faithful and righteous to forgive us our sins and to cleanse us from all unrighteousness"), the cleansing winds of prayer came, blowing your sin away. Once again you were right with God and filled with the Spirit. But look closely. Do you see the alien's legs blowing in the wind? The alien is still clutching the edge of the crevice in your chest with his little suction cup fingers. He remains because the foothold is still there.

James 4:7 says we should submit to God and resist the devil. Submitting to God is not the same as resisting the devil. Jesus was in submission to God, but when the devil attacked him in the wilderness our Lord tapped into "The" power source and verbally commanded the devil, "Begone, satan!" In essence he said "There is authority in my name." Jesus submitted to God but he also spoke words of rebuke toward the enemy (Matthew 4:10). Folks, that's a two-step process and Jesus followed it. No, more than that, Jesus *established* it.

The bottom line is clear: chronic, prolonged behavior in one or more of the categories of sin will produce opportunities for the devil to manifest his influence in your life.

The longer you stay in sin the more opportunity aliens have to attack. And once they are fixed in place, even the prayers of confession won't remove them. Another prayer is required. A warfare prayer. And the result will be deliverance without a lot of hassle.

THE NEXT STEP

Have you ever been angry at another person, God, or yourself for a prolonged period of time?

Did you give away your virginity or have sex with your mate prior to marriage?

Has there been something or someone in your life that has had greater importance to you than Christ?

If so, prepare to check yourself for éclairs in your refrigerator and determine to practice polar bear alerts along the way. Then you can confidently go after your aliens and the footholds that were produced from your sinful past.

Counterattack will take you through the process of submitting to God and resisting the devil in each of the categories of sinful behavior. Up to now the devil's been able to shoot you up pretty good, hasn't he? Kind of like the pig.

WHAT KIND OF FISH ARE YOU?

An excerpt from
Something's Fishy:
Getting Rid of the Carp in Your Life

What kind of fish are you?
CARP
A non-Christian.
BASS
A sold-out, on-fire, goin'-for-it, Jesus lovin' believer.
TROUT
A lukewarm Christian who may or may not be saved. Most people assume trout are saved, but they are either carp or bass dressed to look like trout.

Carp are bottom fish. As they cruise the murky waters, their ugly lips turn downward and play vacuum cleaner, sucking up the stuff that settles. They're scavengers. I think of them as scumsuckers.

In some countries carp are considered a delicacy. But not in the good old U.S. of A. Carp are a trash fish here. I understand why.

Some years ago, a logging company introduced some large goldfishlike carp to a dirty log pond. They thought the carp would clean the lake. They were wrong. In fact, there was a dramatic decline in the brown trout population of the pond. When a heavy rain washed some of the golden boys over the dam, it only took a few months before the local fishermen noticed a rapid demise in the trout population downstream. The carp had taken over. The problem was solved when they introduced bass into the pond and river. Bass beat carp every time . . . they eat the carp fry and so are an effective way to control the carp population.

The moral of the story? When you harbor carp, they quickly take over and drive out the good fish. Carp breed carp.

Most lakes and large rivers contain lots of different fish. But have you noticed, the fewer the carp, the better the fishin' will be? Conversely, the more carp there are, the worse the fishin' will be.

There is something fishy in Christendom and I know what it is: *Carp*. Now I'm not talkin' fish here, I'm talkin' sin . . . deception. I'm talkin' bout people who think they are Christians but aren't. Let me explain.

People call themselves Christians but instead are spawning grounds for carp (sin). In some churches a permissive philosophy is being preached that makes it okay to cultivate the critters. Having a little carp in a life just isn't considered that big of a deal. "I've killed the big ones, and that's good enough," is the attitude of some. Others don't even worry about the big ones. They live life just as they please.

But carp take over . . . they will eat your fry, root you out of church, and mess up your home.

Part of what I'd like to accomplish in this book is to help you get rid of the carp in your life by becoming an aggressive, "kick carp" bass who's sold out to Christ. We'll look at what it takes to become a bass.

Hopefully, by the time you finish this book you will decide for yourself: Which am I?

Am I a carp?

or

Am I a Jesus-lovin', "kick carp" bass?

If you're neither of these, perhaps you'd call yourself a trout. But remember, trout are either carp or bass dressed in trout's clothes. Trout need to wrestle with an important question: Has God drawn lines in the midst of fuzzy gray? Can a fish dressed in trout's clothing really go to heaven?

Carp are a big deal to God. People whose lives are full of carp are middle-of-the-roaders—you can't tell if they are really Christian or not. They live in the middle. Some are, some aren't. Only God knows for sure. If that's you, or someone you know, I hope this book gets your attention.

God got my attention in 1970. That's when he initiated the hunt for carp in my life. I didn't have to look very long. I definitely had a school of 'em swimmin'.

I'll tell you what happened in ***Something's Fishy.***